C0-ARS-135

THE COLLECTED WORKS OF

HENRIK IBSEN

VOLUME X

HEDDA GABLER

THE MASTER BUILDER

THE COLLECTED WORKS OF

HENRIK IBSEN

Copyright Edition. Complete in 11 Volumes
12mo. Price $1.00 each

ENTIRELY REVISED AND EDITED BY

WILLIAM ARCHER

CHARLES SCRIBNER'S SONS

THE COLLECTED WORKS OF
HENRIK IBSEN

COPYRIGHT EDITION

VOLUME X

HEDDA GABLER
THE MASTER BUILDER

TRANSLATED BY
EDMUND GOSSE AND WILLIAM ARCHER

WITH INTRODUCTIONS BY
WILLIAM ARCHER

NEW YORK
CHARLES SCRIBNER'S SONS
1907

CONTENTS

HEDDA GABLER.

INTRODUCTION.*

FROM Munich, on June 29, 1890, Ibsen wrote to the Swedish poet, Count Carl Snoilsky: "Our intention has all along been to spend the summer in the Tyrol again. But circumstances are against our doing so. I am at present engaged upon a new dramatic work, which for several reasons has made very slow progress, and I do not leave Munich until I can take with me the completed first draft. There is little or no prospect of my being able to complete it in July." Ibsen did not leave Munich at all that season. On October 30 he wrote: "At present I am utterly engrossed in a new play. Not one leisure hour have I had for several months." Three weeks later (November 20) he wrote to his French translator, Count Prozor: "My new play is finished; the manuscript went off to Copenhagen the day before yesterday. . . . It produces a curious feeling of emptiness to be thus suddenly separated from a work which has occupied one's time and thoughts for several months, to the exclusion of all else. But it is a good thing, too, to have done with it. The constant intercourse with the fictitious personages was beginning to make me quite nervous." To the same correspondent he wrote on December 4: "The title of the play is *Hedda Gabler.* My intention in giving it this name was to indicate that Hedda, as a personality, is to be regarded rather as her father's daughter than as her husband's wife. It was not my desire to deal in this play with so-called problems. What I principally wanted to do was to depict human beings, human emotions, and human destinies, upon a groundwork of certain of the social conditions and principles of the present day."

So far we read the history of the play in the official "Correspondence."[1] Some interesting glimpses into the poet's moods during the period between the completion of *The Lady from the Sea* and the publication of *Hedda Gabler* are to be found in the series of letters to Fräulein Emilie Bardach, of Vienna, published by Dr. George Brandes.[2] This young lady Ibsen met at Gossensass in the Tyrol in the autumn of 1889. The record of their brief friendship belongs to the history of *The Master Builder* rather than to that of *Hedda Gabler*, but the allusions to his work in his letters to her during the winter of 1889 demand some examination.

So early as October 7, 1889, he writes to her: "A new poem begins to dawn in me. I will execute it this winter, and try to transfer to it the bright atmosphere of the summer. But I feel that it will end in sadness—such is my nature." Was this "dawning" poem *Hedda Gabler*? Or

[1] Letters 214, 216, 217, 219.
[2] In the Ibsen volume of *Die Literatur* (Berlin).

was it rather *The Master Builder* that was germinating in his mind? Who shall say? The latter hypothesis seems the more probable, for it is hard to believe that at any stage in the incubation of *Hedda Gabler* he can have conceived it as even beginning in a key of gaiety. A week later, however, he appears to have made up his mind that the time had not come for the poetic utilisation of his recent experiences. He writes on October 15: "Here I sit as usual at my writing-table. Now I would fain work, but am unable to. My fancy, indeed, is very active. But it always wanders away. It wanders where it has no business to wander during working hours. I cannot repress my summer memories—nor do I wish to. I live through my experiences again and again and yet again. To transmute it all into a poem, I find, in the meantime, impossible." Clearly, then, he felt that his imagination ought to have been engaged on some theme having no relation to his summer experiences—the theme, no doubt, of *Hedda Gabler.* In his next letter, dated October 29, he writes: "Do not be troubled because I cannot, in the meantime, create (*dichten*). In reality I am for ever creating, or, at any rate, dreaming of something which, when in the fulness of time it ripens, will reveal itself as a creation (*Dichtung*)." On November 19 he says: "I am very busily occupied with preparations for my new poem. I sit almost the whole day at my writing-table. Go out only in the evening for a little while." The five following letters contain no allusion to the play; but on September 18, 1890, he wrote: "My wife and son are at present at

Riva, on the Lake of Garda, and will probably remain there until the middle of October, or even longer. Thus I am quite alone here, and cannot get away. The new play on which I am at present engaged will probably not be ready until November, though I sit at my writing-table daily, and almost the whole day long."

Here ends the history of *Hedda Gabler*, so far as the poet's letters carry us. Its hard clear outlines, and perhaps somewhat bleak atmosphere, seem to have resulted from a sort of reaction against the sentimental "dreamery" begotten of his Gossensass experiences. He sought refuge in the chill materialism of Hedda from the ardent transcendentalism of Hilda, whom he already heard knocking at the door. He was not yet in the mood to deal with her on the plane of poetry.[1]

Hedda Gabler was published in Copenhagen on December 16, 1890. This was the first of Ibsen's plays to be translated from proof-sheets and published in England and America almost simultaneously with its first appearance in Scandinavia. The earliest theatrical performance took place at the Residenz Theater, Munich, on the last day of January 1891, in the presence of the poet, Frau Conrad-Ramlo playing the title-part. The Lessing Theater, Berlin, followed suit on February 10. Not till February 25 was the play seen in Copenhagen, with Fru Hennings as Hedda. On the following night it was given

[1] Dr. Julius Elias (*Neue deutsche Rundschau*, December 1906, p. 1462) makes the curious assertion that the character of Thea Elvsted was in part borrowed from this "Gossensasser Hildetypus." It is hard to see how even Ibsen's ingenuity could distil from the same flower two such different essences as Thea and Hilda.

for the first time in Christiania, the Norwegian Hedda being Fröken Constance Bruun. It was this production which the poet saw when he visited the Christiania Theater for the first time after his return to Norway, August 28, 1891. It would take pages to give even the baldest list of the productions and revivals of *Hedda Gabler* in Scandinavia and Germany, where it has always ranked among Ibsen's most popular works. The admirable production of the play by Miss Elizabeth Robins and Miss Marion Lea, at the Vaudeville Theatre, London, April 20, 1891, may rank as the second great step towards the popularisation of Ibsen in England, the first being the Charrington-Achurch production of *A Doll's House* in 1889. Miss Robins afterwards repeated her fine performance of Hedda many times, in London, in the English provinces, and in New York. The character has also been acted in London by Eleonora Duse, and as I write (March 5, 1907) by Mrs. Patrick Campbell, at the Court Theatre. In Australia and America, Hedda has frequently been acted by Miss Nance O'Neill and other actresses — quite recently by a Russian actress, Madame Alla Nazimova, who (playing in English) seems to have made a notable success both in this part and in Nora. The first French Hedda Gabler was Mlle. Marthe Brandès, who played the part at the Vaudeville Theatre, Paris, on December 17, 1891, the performance being introduced by a lecture by M. Jules Lemaître. In Holland, in Italy, in Russia, the play has been acted times without number. In short (as might easily have been foretold) it has rivalled *A Doll's House* in world-wide popularity.

It has been suggested,[1] I think without sufficient ground, that Ibsen deliberately conceived *Hedda Gabler* as an "international" play, and that the scene is really the "west end" of any great European city. To me it seems quite clear that Ibsen had Christiania in mind, and the Christiania of a somewhat earlier period than the 'nineties. The electric cars, telephones, and other conspicuous factors in the life of a modern capital are notably absent from the play. There is no electric light in Secretary Falk's villa. It is still the habit for ladies to return on foot from evening parties, with gallant swains escorting them. This "suburbanism," which so distressed the London critics of 1891, was characteristic of the Christiania Ibsen himself had known in the 'sixties—the Christiania of *Love's Comedy*—rather than of the greatly extended and modernised city of the end of the century. Moreover, Lövborg's allusions to the fiord, and the suggested picture of Sheriff Elvsted, his family and his avocations, are all distinctively Norwegian. The truth seems to be very simple—the environment and the subsidiary personages are all thoroughly national, but Hedda herself is an "international" type, a product of civilisation by no means peculiar to Norway.

We cannot point to any individual model or models who "sat to" Ibsen for the character of Hedda.[2] The late Grant Allen declared that

[1] See article by Herman Bang in *Neue deutsche Rundschau*, December 1906, p. 1495.

[2] Dr. Brahm (*Neue deutsche Rundschau*, December 1906, p. 1422) says that after the first performance of *Hedda Gabler* in Berlin Ibsen confided to him that the character had been suggested by a German lady whom he met in Munich, and who

Hedda was "nothing more nor less than the girl we take down to dinner in London nineteen times out of twenty"; in which case Ibsen must have suffered from a superfluity of models, rather than from any difficulty in finding one. But the fact is that in this, as in all other instances, the word "model" must be taken in a very different sense from that in which it is commonly used in painting. Ibsen undoubtedly used models for this trait and that, but never for a whole figure. If his characters can be called portraits at all, they are composite portraits. Even when it seems pretty clear that the initial impulse towards the creation of a particular character came from some individual, the original figure is entirely transmuted in the process of harmonisation with the dramatic scheme. We need not, therefore, look for a definite prototype of Hedda; but Dr. Brandes shows that two of that lady's exploits were probably suggested by the anecdotic history of the day.

Ibsen had no doubt heard how the wife of a well-known Norwegian composer, in a fit of raging jealousy excited by her husband's prolonged absence from home, burnt the manuscript of a symphony which he had just finished. The circumstances under which Hedda burns Lövborg's manuscript are, of course, entirely different and infinitely more dramatic; but here we have merely another instance of the dramatisation or "poetisation" of the raw material of life. Again, a still more painful incident prob-

did not shoot, but poisoned herself. Nothing more seems to be known of this lady. See, too, an article by Julius Elias in the same magazine, p. 1460.

ably came to his knowledge about the same time. A beautiful and very intellectual woman was married to a well-known man who had been addicted to drink, but had entirely conquered the vice. One day a mad whim seized her to put his self-mastery and her power over him to the test. As it happened to be his birthday, she rolled into his study a small keg of brandy, and then withdrew. She returned some time afterwards to find that he had broached the keg, and lay insensible on the floor. In this anecdote we cannot but recognise the germ, not only of Hedda's temptation of Lövborg, but of a large part of her character.

"Thus," says Dr. Brandes, "out of small and scattered traits of reality Ibsen fashioned his close-knit and profoundly thought-out works of art."

For the character of Eilert Lövborg, again, Ibsen seems unquestionably to have borrowed several traits from a definite original. A young Danish man of letters, whom Dr. Brandes calls Holm, was an enthusiastic admirer of Ibsen, and came to be on very friendly terms with him. One day Ibsen was astonished to receive, in Munich, a parcel addressed from Berlin by this young man, containing, without a word of explanation, a packet of his (Ibsen's) letters, and a photograph which he had presented to Holm. Ibsen brooded and brooded over the incident, and at last came to the conclusion that the young man had intended to return her letters and photograph to a young lady to whom he was known to be attached, and had in a fit of aberration mixed up the two objects of his worship.

Some time after, Holm appeared at Ibsen's rooms. He talked quite rationally, but professed to have no knowledge whatever of the letter-incident, though he admitted the truth of Ibsen's conjecture that the "belle dame sans merci" had demanded the return of her letters and portrait. Ibsen was determined to get at the root of the mystery; and a little inquiry into his young friend's habits revealed the fact that he broke his fast on a bottle of port wine, consumed a bottle of Rhine wine at lunch, of Burgundy at dinner, and finished off the evening with one or two more bottles of port. Then he heard, too, how, in the course of a night's carouse, Holm had lost the manuscript of a book; and in these traits he saw the outline of the figure of Eilert Lövborg.

Some time elapsed, and again Ibsen received a postal packet from Holm. This one contained his will, in which Ibsen figured as his residuary legatee. But many other legatees were mentioned in the instrument—all of them ladies, such as Fräulein Alma Rothbart, of Bremen, and Fräulein Elise Kraushaar, of Berlin. The bequests to these meritorious spinsters were so generous that their sum considerably exceeded the amount of the testator's property. Ibsen gently but firmly declined the proffered inheritance; but Holm's will no doubt suggested to him the figure of that red-haired "Mademoiselle Diana," who is heard of but not seen in *Hedda Gabler*, and enabled him to add some further traits to the portraiture of Lövborg. When the play appeared, Holm recognised himself with glee in the character of the bibulous man of letters, and thereafter adopted "Eilert Lövborg" as his pseudonym. I do not, therefore, see why Dr. Brandes should suppress his real name; but I willingly imitate him in erring on the side of discretion. The poor fellow died several years ago.

Some critics have been greatly troubled as to the precise meaning of Hedda's fantastic vision of Lövborg "with vine-leaves in his hair." Surely this is a very obvious image or symbol of the beautiful, the ideal, aspect of bacchic elation and revelry. Antique art, or I am much mistaken, shows us many figures of Dionysus himself and his followers with vine-leaves entwined in their hair. To Ibsen's mind, at any rate, the image had long been familiar. In *Peer Gynt* (Act iv. sc. 8), when Peer, having carried off Anitra, finds himself in a particularly festive mood, he cries: "Were there vine-leaves around, I would garland my brow." Again, in *Emperor and Galilean* (Pt. ii. Act 1) where Julian, in the procession of Dionysus, impersonates the god himself, it is directed that he shall wear a wreath of vine-leaves. Professor Dietrichson relates that among the young artists whose society Ibsen frequented during his first years in Rome, it was customary, at their little festivals, for the revellers to deck themselves in this fashion. But the image is so obvious that there is no need to trace it to any personal experience. The attempt to place Hedda's vine-leaves among Ibsen's obscurities is an example of the firm resolution not to understand which animated the criticism of the 'nineties.

Dr. Brandes has dealt very severely with the

character of Eilert Lövborg, alleging that we cannot believe in the genius attributed to him. But where is he described as a genius? The poet represents him as a very able student of sociology; but that is a quite different thing from attributing to him such genius as must necessarily shine forth in every word he utters. Dr. Brandes, indeed, declines to believe even in his ability as a sociologist, on the ground that it is idle to write about the social development of the future. "To our prosaic minds," he says, "it may seem as if the most sensible utterance on the subject is that of the fool of the play: 'The future! Good heavens, we know nothing of the future.'" The best retort to this criticism is that which Eilert himself makes: "There's a thing or two to be said about it all the same." The intelligent forecasting of the future (as Mr. H. G. Wells has shown) is not only clearly distinguishable from fantastic Utopianism, but is indispensable to any large statesmanship or enlightened social activity. With very real and very great respect for Dr. Brandes, I cannot think that he has been fortunate in his treatment of Lövborg's character. It has been represented as an absurdity that he should think of reading abstracts from his new book to a man like Tesman, whom he despises. But though Tesman is a ninny, he is, as Hedda says, a "specialist"—he is a competent, plodding student of his subject. Lövborg may quite naturally wish to see how his new method, or his excursion into a new field, strikes the average scholar of the Tesman type. He is, in fact, "trying it on the dog"—neither an unreasonable nor an unusual proceeding. There is, no doubt, a certain improbability in the way in which Lövborg is represented as carrying his manuscript around, and especially in Mrs. Elvsted's production of his rough draft from her pocket; but these are mechanical trifles, on which only a niggling criticism would dream of laying stress.

Of all Ibsen's works, *Hedda Gabler* is the most detached, the most objective—a character-study pure and simple. It is impossible—or so it seems to me—to extract any sort of general idea from it. One cannot even call it a satire, unless one is prepared to apply that term to the record of a "case" in a work on criminology. Reverting to Dumas's dictum that a play should contain "a painting, a judgment, an ideal," we may say that *Hedda Gabler* fulfils only the first of these requirements. The poet does not even pass judgment on his heroine: he simply paints her full-length portrait with scientific impassivity. But what a portrait! How searching in insight, how brilliant in colouring, how rich in detail! Grant Allen's remark, above quoted, was, of course, a whimsical exaggeration: the Hedda type is not so common as all that, else the world would quickly come to an end. But particular traits and tendencies of the Hedda type are very common in modern life, and not only among women. Hyperæsthesia lies at the root of her tragedy. With a keenly critical, relentlessly solvent intelligence, she combines a morbid shrinking from all the gross and prosaic detail of the sensual life. She has nothing to take her out of herself—not a single intellectual interest or moral enthusiasm. She cherishes, in a languid way, a petty social ambition; and even that she finds obstructed and baffled. At the same time she learns that another woman has had the courage to love and venture all, where she, in her cowardice, only hankered and refrained. Her malign egoism rises up uncontrolled, and calls to its aid her quick and subtle intellect. She ruins the other woman's happiness, but in doing so incurs a danger from which her sense of personal dignity revolts. Life has no such charm for her that she cares to purchase it at the cost of squalid humiliation and self-contempt. The good and the bad in her alike impel her to have done with it all; and a pistol-shot ends what is surely one of the most poignant character-tragedies in literature. Ibsen's brain never worked at higher pressure than in the conception and adjustment of those "crowded hours" in which Hedda, tangled in the web of Will and Circumstance, struggles on till she is too weary to struggle any more.

It may not be superfluous to note that the "a" in "Gabler" should be sounded long and full, like the "a" in "garden"—*not* like the "a" in "gable" or in "gabble."

W. A.

THE MASTER BUILDER.

INTRODUCTION.*

WITH *The Master Builder*—or *Master Builder Solness*, as the title runs in the original—we enter upon the final stage in Ibsen's career. "You are essentially right," the poet wrote to Count Prozor in March 1900, "when you say that the series which closes with the Epilogue (*When We Dead Awaken*) began with *Master Builder Solness*."

"Ibsen," says Dr. Brahm, "wrote in Christiania all the four works which he thus seems to bracket together—*Solness*, *Eyolf*, *Borkman*, and *When We Dead Awaken*. He returned to Norway in July 1891, for a stay of indefinite length; but the restless wanderer over Europe was destined to leave his home no more. . . . He had not returned, however, to throw himself, as of old, into the battle of the passing day. Polemics are entirely absent from the poetry of his old age. He leaves the State and Society at peace. He who had departed as the creator of Falk [in *Love's Comedy*] now, on his return, gazes, not satirically, but rather in a lyric mood, into the secret places of human nature and the wonders of his own soul."

Dr. Brahm, however, seems to be mistaken in thinking that Ibsen returned to Norway with no definite intention of settling down. Dr. Julius Elias (an excellent authority) reports that shortly before Ibsen left Munich in 1891, he remarked one day, "I must get back to the North!" "Is that a sudden impulse?" asked Elias. "Oh no," was the reply; "I want to be a good head of a household and have my affairs in order. To that end I must consolidate my property, lay it down in good securities, and get it under control—and that one can best do where one has rights of citizenship." Some critics will no doubt be shocked to find the poet whom they have written down an "anarchist" confessing such bourgeois motives.

After his return to Norway, Ibsen's correspondence became very scant, and we have no letters dating from the period when he was at work on *The Master Builder*. On the other hand, we possess a curious lyrical prelude to the play, which he put on paper on March 16, 1892. It is said to have been his habit, before setting to work on a play, to "crystallise in a poem the mood which then possessed him;" but the following is the only one of these keynote poems which has been published. I give it in the original language, with a literal translation:

DE SAD DER, DE TO—

De sad der, de to, i saa lunt et hus
ved höst og i vinterdage,
Saa brændte huset. Alt ligger i grus.
De to faar i asken rage.

For nede i den er et smykke gemt,—
et smykke, som aldrig kan brænde.

Og leder de trofast, hænder det nemt
at det findes af ham eller hende.

Men finder de end, de brandlidte to,
det dyre, ildfaste smykke,—
aldrig h n finder sin brændte tro,
han aldrig sin brændte lykke.

THEY SAT THERE, THE TWO—

They sat there, the two, in so cosy a house, through autumn and winter days. Then the house burned down. Everything lies in ruins. The two must grope among the ashes.

For among them is hidden a jewel—a jewel that never can burn. And if they search faithfully, it may easily happen that he or she may find it.

But even should they find it, the burnt-out two—find this precious unburnable jewel—never will *she* find her burnt faith, *he* never his burnt happiness.

This is the latest piece of Ibsen's verse that has been given to the world; but one of his earliest poems—first printed in 1858—was also, in some sort, a prelude to *The Master Builder*. Of this a literal translation may suffice. It is called

BUILDING-PLANS

I remember as clearly as if it had been to-day the evening when, in the paper, I saw my first poem in print. There I sat in my den, and, with long-drawn puffs, I smoked and I dreamed in blissful self-complacency.

"I will build a cloud-castle. It shall shine all over the North. It shall have two wings: one little and one great. The great wing shall shelter a deathless poet; the little wing shall serve as a young girl's bower."

The plan seemed to me nobly harmonious; but as time went on it fell into confusion. When the master grew reasonable, the castle turned utterly crazy; the great wing became too little, the little wing fell to ruin.

Thus we see that, thirty-five years before the date of *The Master Builder*, Ibsen's imagination was preoccupied with a symbol of a master building a castle in the air, and a young girl in one of its towers.

There has been some competition among the poet's young lady friends for the honour of having served as his model for Hilda. Several, no doubt, are entitled to some share in it. One is not surprised to learn that among the papers he left behind were sheaves upon sheaves of letters from women. "All these ladies," says Dr. Julius Elias, "demanded something of him—some cure for their agonies of soul, or for the incomprehension from which they suffered; some solution of the riddle of their nature. Almost every one of them regarded herself as a problem to which Ibsen could not but have the time and the interest to apply himself. They all thought they had a claim on the creator of Nora. . . . Of this chapter of his experience, Fru Ibsen spoke with ironic humour. 'Ibsen (I have often said to him), Ibsen, keep these swarms of over-strained womenfolk at arm's length.' 'Oh no (he would reply), let them alone. I want to observe them more closely.' His observations would take a longer or shorter time as the case might be, and would always contribute to some work of art."

The principal model for Hilda was doubtless Fräulein Emilie Bardach, of Vienna, whom he met at Gossensass in the autumn of 1889. He was then sixty-one years of age; she is said to have been seventeen. As the lady herself handed his letters to Dr. Brandes for publication, there can be no indiscretion in speaking of them freely. Some passages from them I have quoted in the introduction to *Hedda Gabler*—passages which show that at first the poet deliberately put aside his Gossensass impressions for use when he should stand at a greater distance from them, and meanwhile devoted himself to work in a totally different key. On October 15, 1889, he writes, in his second letter to Fräulein Bardach: "I cannot repress my summer memories, nor do I want to. I live through my experiences again and again, and yet again. To transmute it all into a poem I find, in the meantime, impossible. In the meantime? Shall I succeed in doing so some time in the future? And do I really wish to succeed? In the meantime, at any rate, I do not. . . . And yet it must come in time." The letters number twelve in all, and are couched in a tone of sentimental regret for the brief, bright summer days of their acquaintanceship. The keynote is struck in the inscription on the back of a photograph which he gave her before they parted: *An die Maisonne eines Septemberlebens —in Tirol*,[1] 27/9/89. In her album he had written the words:

> Hohes, schmerzliches Glück—
> um das Unerreichbare zu ringen![2]

in which we may, if we like, see a foreshadowing of the Solness frame of mind. In the fifth letter of the series he refers to her as "an enigmatic Princess"; in the sixth he twice calls her "my dear Princess"; but this is the only point at which the letters quite definitely and unmistakably point forward to *The Master Builder*.

[1] "To the May-sun of a September life—in Tyrol."

[2] "High, painful happiness—to struggle for the unattainable!"

In the ninth letter (February 6, 1890) he says: "I feel it a matter of conscience to end, or at any rate, to restrict, our correspondence." The tenth letter, six months later, is one of kindly condolence on the death of the young lady's father. In the eleventh (very short) note, dated December 30, 1890, he acknowledges some small gift, but says: "Please, for the present, do not write to me again. . . . I will soon send you my new play [*Hedda Gabler*]. Receive it in friendship, but in silence!" This injunction she apparently obeyed. When *The Master Builder* appeared, it would seem that Ibsen did not even send her a copy of the play; and we gather that he was rather annoyed when she sent him a photograph signed "Princess of Orangia." On his seventieth birthday, however, she telegraphed her congratulations, to which he returned a very cordial reply. And here their relations ended.

That she was right, however, in regarding herself as his principal model for Hilda appears from an anecdote related by Dr. Elias.[1] It is not an altogether pleasing anecdote, but Dr. Elias is an unexceptionable witness, and it can by no means be omitted from an examination into the origins of *The Master Builder*. Ibsen had come to Berlin in February 1891 for the first performance of *Hedda Gabler*. Such experiences were always a trial to him, and he felt greatly relieved when they were over. Packing, too, he detested; and Elias having helped him through this terrible ordeal, the two sat down to lunch together, while awaiting the train. An expansive mood descended upon Ibsen, and chuc-

[1] *Neue deutsche Rundschau*, December, 1906, p. 1462.

kling over his champagne glass, he said: "Do you know, my next play is already hovering before me—of course in vague outline. But of one thing I have got firm hold. An experience: a woman's figure. Very interesting, very interesting indeed. Again a spice of devilry in it." Then he related how he had met in the Tyrol a Viennese girl of very remarkable character. She had at once made him her confidant. The gist of her confessions was that she did not care a bit about one day marrying a well brought-up young man—most likely she would never marry. What tempted and charmed and delighted her was to lure other women's husbands away from them. She was a little dæmonic wrecker; she often appeared to him like a little bird of prey, that would fain have made him, too, her booty. He had studied her very, very closely. For the rest, she had had no great success with him. "She did not get hold of me, but I got hold of her—for my play. Then I fancy" (here he chuckled again) "she consoled herself with some one else." Love seemed to mean for her only a sort of morbid imagination. This, however, was only one side of her nature. His little model had had a great deal of heart and of womanly understanding; and thanks to the spontaneous power she could gain over him, every woman might, if she wished it, guide some man towards the good. "Thus Ibsen spoke," says Elias, "calmly and coolly, gazing as it were into the far distance, like an artist taking an objective view of some experience—like Lubek speaking of his soul-thefts. He had stolen a soul, and put it to a double employment. Thea Elvsted and

Hilda Wangel are intimately related—are, indeed, only different expressions of the same nature." If Ibsen actually declared Thea and Hilda to be drawn from one model, we must of course take his word for it; but the relationship is hard to discern.

There can be no reasonable doubt, then, that the Gossensass episode gave the primary impulse to *The Master Builder*. But it seems pretty well established, too, that another lady, whom he met in Christiania after his return in 1891, also contributed largely to the character of Hilda. This may have been the reason why he resented Fräulein Bardach's appropriating to herself the title of "Princess of Orangia."

The play was published in the middle of December 1892. It was acted both in Germany and England before it was seen in the Scandinavian capitals. Its first performance took place at the Lessing Theatre, Berlin, January 19, 1893, with Emanuel Reicher as Solness and Frl. Reisenhofer as Hilda. In London it was first performed at the Trafalgar Square Theatre (now the Duke of York's) on February 20, 1893, under the direction of Mr. Herbert Waring and Miss Elizabeth Robins, who played Solness and Hilda. This was one of the most brilliant and successful of English Ibsen productions. Miss Robins was almost an ideal Hilda, and Mr. Waring's Solness was exceedingly able. Some thirty performances were given in all, and the play was reproduced at the Opera Comique later in the season, with Mr. Lewis Waller as Solness. In the following year Miss Robins acted Hilda in Manchester. In Christiania and Copenhagen the play was produced on the same evening, March 8, 1893; the Copenhagen Solness and Hilda were Emil Poulsen and Fru Hennings. A Swedish production, by Lindberg, soon followed, both in Stockholm and Gothenburg. In Paris *Solness le constructeur* was not seen until April 3, 1894, when it was produced by "L'Œuvre" with M. Lugné-Poë as Solness. This company, sometimes with Mme. Suzanne Desprès and sometimes with Mme. Berthe Bady as Hilda, in 1894 and 1895 presented the play in London, Brussels, Amsterdam, Milan, and other cities. In October 1894 they visited Christiania, where Ibsen was present at one of their performances, and is reported by Herman Bang to have been so enraptured with it that he exclaimed, "This is the resurrection of my play!" On this occasion Mme. Bady was the Hilda. The first performance of the play in America took place at the Carnegie Lyceum, New York, on January 16, 1900, with Mr. William H. Pascoe as Solness and Miss Florence Kahn as Hilda. The performance was repeated in the course of the same month, both at Washington and Boston.

In England, and probably elsewhere as well, *The Master Builder* produced a curious double effect. It alienated many of the poet's staunchest admirers, and it powerfully attracted many people who had hitherto been hostile to him. Looking back, it is easy to see why this should have been so; for here was certainly a new thing in drama, which could not but set up many novel reactions. A greater contrast could scarcely be imagined than that between the hard, cold, precise outlines of *Hedda Gabler* and the vague mysterious atmosphere of *The Master Builder*, in which, though the dialogue is sternly restrained within the limits of prose, the art of drama seems for ever on the point of floating away to blend with the art of music. Substantially, the play is one long dialogue between Solness and Hilda; and it would be quite possible to analyse this dialogue in terms of music, noting (for example) the announcement first of this theme and then of that, the resumption and reinforcement of a theme which seemed to have been dropped, the contrapuntal interweaving of two or more motives, a scherzo here, a fugal passage there. Leaving this exercise to some one more skilled in music (or less unskilled) than myself, I may note that in *The Master Builder* Ibsen resumes his favourite retrospective method, from which in *Hedda Gabler* he had in great measure departed. But the retrospect with which we are here concerned is purely psychological. The external events involved in it are few and simple in comparison with the external events which are successively unveiled in the retrospective passages of *The Wild Duck* or *Rosmersholm*. The matter of the play is the soul-history of Halvard Solness, recounted to an impassioned listener—so impassioned, indeed, that the soul-changes it begets in her form an absorbing and thrilling drama. The graduations, retardations, accelerations of Solness's self-revealment are managed with the subtlest art, so as to keep the interest of the spectator ever on the stretch. The technical method was not new; it was simply that which Ibsen had been perfecting from *Pillars of Society* onward; but it was applied to a subject of a nature not only new to him, but new to literature.

That the play is full of symbolism it would be futile to deny; and the symbolism is mainly autobiographic. The churches which Solness sets out by building doubtless represent Ibsen's early romantic plays, the "homes for human beings" his social dramas; while the houses with high towers, merging into "castles in the air," stand for those spiritual dramas, with a wide outlook over the metaphysical environment of humanity, on which he was henceforth to be engaged. Perhaps it is not altogether fanciful to read a personal reference into Solness's refusal to call himself an architect, on the ground that his training has not been systematic—that he is a self-taught man. Ibsen too was in all essentials self-taught; his philosophy was entirely unsystematic; and, like Solness, he was no student of books. There may be an introspective note also in that dread of the younger generation to which Solness confesses. It is certain that the old Master-Builder was not lavish of his certificates of competence to young aspirants, though there is nothing to show that his reticence ever depressed or quenched any rising genius.

On the whole, then, it cannot be doubted that several symbolic motives are inwoven into the iridescent fabric of the play. But it is a great mistake to regard it as essentially and inseparably a piece of symbolism. Essentially it is history of a sickly conscience, worked out in terms of pure psychology. Or rather, it is a study of a sickly and a robust conscience side by side. "The conscience is very conservative," Ibsen has somewhere said; and here Solness's conservatism is contrasted with Hilda's radicalism—or rather would-be radicalism, for we are led to suspect, towards the close, that the radical too is a conservative in spite of herself. The fact that Solness cannot climb as high as he builds implies, I take it, that he cannot act as freely as he thinks, or as Hilda would goad him into thinking. At such an altitude his conscience would turn dizzy, and life would become impossible to him. But here I am straying back to the interpretation of symbols. My present purpose is to insist that there is nothing in the play which has no meaning on the natural-psychological plane, and absolutely requires a symbolic interpretation to make it comprehensible. The symbols are harmonic undertones; the psychological melody is clear and consistent without any reference to them.[1] It is true that, in order to accept the action on what we may call the realistic level, we must suppose Solness to possess and to exercise, sometimes in spite of himself, and sometimes unconsciously, a considerable measure of hypnotic power. But the time is surely past when we could reckon hypnotism among "supernatural" phenomena. Whether

[1] This conception I have worked out at much greater length in an essay, entitled *The Melody of the Master Builder*, appended to the shilling edition of the play, published in 1893. I there retell the story, transplanting it to England and making the hero a journalist instead of an architect, in order to show that (if we grant the reality of certain commonly-accepted phenomena of hypnotism) there is nothing incredible or even extravagantly improbable about it. The argument is far too long to be included here, but the reader who is interested in the subject may find it worth referring to.

the particular forms of hypnotic influence attributed to Solness do actually exist is a question we need not determine. The poet does not demand our absolute credence, as though he were giving evidence in the witness-box. What he requires is our imaginative acceptance of certain incidents which he purposely leaves hovering on the border between the natural and the preternatural, the explained and the unexplained. In this play, as in *The Lady from the Sea* and *Little Eyolf*, he shows a delicacy of art in his dalliance with the occult which irresistibly recalls the exquisite genius of Nathaniel Hawthorne.[1]

The critics who insist on finding nothing but symbolism in the play have fastened on Mrs. Solness's "nine lovely dolls," and provided the most amazing interpretations for them. A letter which I contributed in 1893 to the *Westminster Gazette* records an incident which throws a curious light on the subject, and may be worth preserving. "At a recent first night," I wrote, "I happened to be seated just behind a well-known critic. He turned round to me and said, 'I want you to tell me what is *your* theory of those "nine lovely dolls." Of course one can see that they are entirely symbolical.' 'I am not so sure of that,' I replied, remembering a Norwegian cousin of my own who treasured a favourite doll until she was nearer thirty than twenty. 'They of course symbolise the unsatisfied passion of motherhood in Mrs. Solness's heart, but I have

[1] For an instance of the technical methods by which he suggested the supernormal element in the atmosphere of the play, see Introduction to *A Doll's House*, p. xiv.

very little doubt that Ibsen makes use of this "symbol" because he has observed a similar case, or cases, in real life.' 'What!' cried the critic. 'He has seen a grown-up, a middle-aged, woman continuing to "live with" her dolls!' I was about to say that it did not seem to me so very improbable, when a lady who was seated next me, a total stranger to both of us, leant forward and said, 'Excuse my interrupting you, but it may perhaps interest you to know that *I have three dolls to which I am deeply attached!'* I will not be so rude as to conjecture this lady's age, but we may be sure that a very young woman would not have had the courage to make such an avowal. Does it not seem that Ibsen knows a thing or two about human nature—English as well as Norwegian—which we dramatic critics, though bound by our calling to be subtle psychologists, have not yet fathomed?" In the course of the correspondence which followed, one very apposite anecdote was quoted from an American paper, the *Argonaut:* "An old Virginia lady said to a friend, on finding a treasured old cup cracked by a careless maid, 'I know of nothing to compare with the affliction of losing a handsome piece of old china.' 'Surely,' said the friend, 'it is not so bad as losing one's children.' 'Yes, it is,' replied the old lady, 'for when your children die, you do have the consolations of religion, you know.'"

It would be a paradox to call *The Master Builder* Ibsen's greatest work, but one of his three or four greatest it assuredly is. Of all his writings, it is probably the most original, the most individual, the most unlike any other drama by any other writer. The form of *Brand* and *Peer Gynt* was doubtless suggested by other dramatic poems — notably by *Faust*. In *The Wild Duck*, in *Rosmersholm*, in *Hedda Gabler*, even in *Little Eyolf* and *John Gabriel Borkman*, there remain faint traces of the French leaven which was so strong in the earlier plays. But *The Master Builder* had no model and has no parallel. It shows no slightest vestige of outside influence. It is Ibsen, and nothing but Ibsen.

W. A.

HEDDA GABLER

(1890)

VOL. X.

CHARACTERS.

GEORGE TESMAN.[1]
HEDDA TESMAN, *his wife.*
MISS JULIANA TESMAN, *his aunt.*
MRS. ELVSTED.
JUDGE[2] BRACK.
EILERT LÖVBORG.
BERTA, *servant at the Tesmans.*

The scene of the action is Tesman's villa, in the west end of Christiania.

[1] Tesman, whose Christian name in the original is "Jörgen," is described as "stipendiat i kulturhistorie"—that is to say, the holder of a scholarship for purposes of research into the History of Civilisation.
[2] In the original "Assessor."

HEDDA GABLER.

PLAY IN FOUR ACTS.

ACT FIRST.

A spacious, handsome, and tastefully furnished drawing-room, decorated in dark colours. In the back, a wide doorway with curtains drawn back, leading into a smaller room decorated in the same style as the drawing-room. In the right-hand wall of the front room, a folding door leading out to the hall. In the opposite wall, on the left, a glass door, also with curtains drawn back. Through the panes can be seen part of a veranda outside, and trees covered with autumn foliage. An oval table, with a cover on it, and surrounded by chairs, stands well forward. In front, by the wall on the right, a wide stove of dark porcelain, a high-backed arm-chair, a cushioned foot-rest, and two footstools. A settee, with a small round table in front of it, fills the upper right-hand corner. In front, on the left, a little way from the wall, a sofa. Further back than the glass door, a piano. On either side of the doorway at the back a what-not with terra-cotta and majolica ornaments.—Against the back wall of the inner room a sofa, with a table, and one or two chairs. Over the sofa hangs the portrait of a handsome elderly man in a General's uniform. Over the table a hanging lamp, with an opal glass shade.—A number of bouquets are arranged about the drawing-room, in vases and glasses. Others lie upon the tables. The floors in both rooms are covered with thick carpets.—Morning light. The sun shines in through the glass door.

MISS JULIANA TESMAN, *with her bonnet on and carrying a parasol, comes in from the hall, followed by* BERTA, *who carries a bouquet wrapped in paper.* MISS TESMAN *is a comely and pleasant-looking lady of about sixty-five. She is nicely but simply dressed in a grey walking-costume.* BERTA *is a middle-aged woman of plain and rather countrified appearance.*

MISS TESMAN.

[*Stops close to the door, listens, and says softly* :] Upon my word, I don't believe they are stirring yet!

BERTA.

[*Also softly.*] I told you so, Miss. Remember how late the steamboat got in last night. And then, when they got home!—good Lord, what a lot the young mistress had to unpack before she could get to bed.

MISS TESMAN.

Well well—let them have their sleep out. But let us see that they get a good breath of the fresh morning air when they do appear.

[*She goes to the glass door and throws it open.*

BERTA.

[*Beside the table, at a loss what to do with the bouquet in her hand.*] I declare there isn't a bit of room left. I think I'll put it down here, Miss.

[*She places it on the piano.*

MISS TESMAN.

So you've got a new mistress now, my dear Berta. Heaven knows it was a wrench to me to part with you.

BERTA.

[*On the point of weeping.*] And do you think it wasn't hard for me too, Miss? After all the blessed years I've been with you and Miss Rina.[1]

MISS TESMAN.

We must make the best of it, Berta. There was nothing else to be done. George can't do without you, you see—he absolutely can't. He has had you to look after him ever since he was a little boy.

BERTA.

Ah but, Miss Julia, I can't help thinking of Miss Rina lying helpless at home there, poor thing. And with only that new girl too! She'll never learn to take proper care of an invalid.

MISS TESMAN.

Oh, I shall manage to train her. And of course, you know, I shall take most of it upon myself. You needn't be uneasy about my poor sister, my dear Berta.

[1] Pronounce *Reena.*

BERTA.

Well, but there's another thing, Miss. I'm so mortally afraid I shan't be able to suit the young mistress.

MISS TESMAN.

Oh well—just at first there may be one or two things——

BERTA.

Most like she'll be terrible grand in her ways.

MISS TESMAN.

Well, you can't wonder at that—General Gabler's daughter! Think of the sort of life she was accustomed to in her father's time. Don't you remember how we used to see her riding down the road along with the General? In that long black habit—and with feathers in her hat?

BERTA.

Yes indeed—I remember well enough!—But, good Lord, I should never have dreamt in those days that she and Master George would make a match of it.

MISS TESMAN.

Nor I.—But by-the-bye, Berta—while I think of it: in future you mustn't say Master George. You must say Dr. Tesman.

BERTA.

Yes, the young mistress spoke of that too—last night—the moment they set foot in the house. Is it true then, Miss?

MISS TESMAN.

Yes, indeed it is. Only think, Berta—some

foreign university has made him a doctor—while he has been abroad, you understand. I hadn't heard a word about it, until he told me himself upon the pier.

BERTA.

Well well, he's clever enough for anything, he is. But I didn't think he'd have gone in for doctoring people too.

MISS TESMAN.

No no, it's not that sort of doctor he is. [*Nods significantly.*] But let me tell you, we may have to call him something still grander before long.

BERTA.

You don't say so! What can that be, Miss?

MISS TESMAN.

[*Smiling.*] H'm—wouldn't you like to know! [*With emotion.*] Ah, dear dear—if my poor brother could only look up from his grave now, and see what his little boy has grown into! [*Looks around.*] But bless me, Berta—why have you done this? Taken the chintz covers off all the furniture?

BERTA.

The mistress told me to. She can't abide covers on the chairs, she says.

MISS TESMAN.

Are they going to make this their everyday sitting-room then?

BERTA.

Yes, that's what I understood—from the mistress. Master George—the doctor—he said nothing.

GEORGE TESMAN *comes from the right into the inner room, humming to himself, and carrying an unstrapped empty portmanteau. He is a middle-sized, young-looking man of thirty-three, rather stout, with a round, open, cheerful face, fair hair and beard. He wears spectacles, and is somewhat carelessly dressed in comfortable indoor clothes.*

MISS TESMAN.

Good morning, good morning, George.

TESMAN.

[*In the doorway between the rooms.*] Aunt Julia! Dear Aunt Julia! [*Goes up to her and shakes hands warmly.*] Come all this way—so early! Eh?

MISS TESMAN.

Why, of course I had to come and see how you were getting on.

TESMAN.

In spite of your having had no proper night's rest?

MISS TESMAN.

Oh, that makes no difference to me.

TESMAN.

Well, I suppose you got home all right from the pier? Eh?

MISS TESMAN.

Yes, quite safely, thank goodness. Judge Brack was good enough to see me right to my door.

TESMAN.

We were so sorry we couldn't give you a seat in

the carriage. But you saw what a pile of boxes Hedda had to bring with her.

MISS TESMAN.

Yes, she had certainly plenty of boxes.

BERTA.

[*To* TESMAN.] Shall I go in and see if there's anything I can do for the mistress?

TESMAN.

No thank you, Berta—you needn't. She said she would ring if she wanted anything.

BERTA.

[*Going towards the right.*] Very well.

TESMAN.

But look here—take this portmanteau with you.

BERTA.

[*Taking it.*] I'll put it in the attic.

[*She goes out by the hall door*

TESMAN.

Fancy, Auntie—I had the whole of that portmanteau chock full of copies of documents. You wouldn't believe how much I have picked up from all the archives I have been examining—curious old details that no one has had any idea of——

MISS TESMAN.

Yes, you don't seem to have wasted your time on your wedding trip, George.

TESMAN.

No, that I haven't. But do take off your bonnet, Auntie. Look here! Let me untie the strings—eh?

MISS TESMAN.

[*While he does so.*] Well well—this is just as if you were still at home with us.

TESMAN.

[*With the bonnet in his hand, looks at it from all sides.*] Why, what a gorgeous bonnet you've been investing in!

MISS TESMAN.

I bought it on Hedda's account.

TESMAN.

On Hedda's account? Eh?

MISS TESMAN.

Yes, so that Hedda needn't be ashamed of me if we happened to go out together.

TESMAN.

[*Patting her cheek.*] You always think of everything, Aunt Julia. [*Lays the bonnet on a chair beside the table.*] And now, look here—suppose we sit comfortably on the sofa and have a little chat, till Hedda comes.

[*They seat themselves. She places her parasol in the corner of the sofa.*

MISS TESMAN.

[*Takes both his hands and looks at him.*] What a delight it is to have you again, as large as life, before my very eyes, George! My George—my p oorbrother's own boy!

TESMAN.

And it's a delight for me, too, to see you again, Aunt Julia! You, who have been father and mother in one to me.

MISS TESMAN.

Oh yes, I know you will always keep a place in your heart for your old aunts.

TESMAN.

And what about Aunt Rina? No improvement —eh?

MISS TESMAN.

Oh no—we can scarcely look for any improvement in her case, poor thing. There she lies, helpless, as she has lain for all these years. But heaven grant I may not lose her yet awhile: For if I did, I don't know what I should make of my life, George—especially now that I haven't you to look after any more.

TESMAN.

[*Patting her back.*] There there there——!

MISS TESMAN.

[*Suddenly changing her tone.*] And to think that here are you a married man, George!—And that you should be the one to carry off Hedda Gabler —the beautiful Hedda Gabler! Only think of it —she, that was so beset with admirers!

TESMAN.

[*Hums a little and smiles complacently.*] Yes, I fancy I have several good friends about town who would like to stand in my shoes—eh?

MISS TESMAN.

And then this fine long wedding-tour you have had! More than five—nearly six months——

TESMAN.

Well, for me it has been a sort of tour of research as well. I have had to do so much grubbing among old records—and to read no end of books too, Auntie.

MISS TESMAN.

Oh yes, I suppose so. [*More confidentially, and lowering her voice a little.*] But listen now, George,—have you nothing—nothing special to tell me?

TESMAN.

As to our journey?

MISS TESMAN.

Yes.

TESMAN.

No, I don't know of anything except what I have told you in my letters. I had a doctor's degree conferred on me—but that I told you yesterday.

MISS TESMAN.

Yes, yes, you did. But what I mean is—haven't you any—any—expectations——?

TESMAN.

Expectations?

MISS TESMAN.

Why you know, George—I'm your old auntie!

TESMAN.

Why, of course I have expectations.

MISS TESMAN.

Ah!

TESMAN.

I have every expectation of being a professor one of these days.

MISS TESMAN.

Oh yes, a professor——

TESMAN.

Indeed, I may say I am certain of it. But my dear Auntie—you know all about that already!

MISS TESMAN.

[*Laughing to herself.*] Yes, of course I do. You are quite right there. [*Changing the subject.*] But we were talking about your journey. It must have cost a great deal of money, George?

TESMAN.

Well, you see—my handsome travelling-scholarship went a good way.

MISS TESMAN.

But I can't understand how you can have made it go far enough for two.

TESMAN.

No, that's not so easy to understand—eh?

MISS TESMAN.

And especially travelling with a lady—they tell me that makes it ever so much more expensive.

TESMAN.

Yes, of course—it makes it a little more expensive. But Hedda had to have this trip, Auntie! She really had to. Nothing else would have done.

MISS TESMAN.

No no, I suppose not. A wedding-tour seems to be quite indispensable nowadays.—But tell me now —have you gone thoroughly over the house yet?

TESMAN.

Yes, you may be sure I have. I have been afoot ever since daylight.

MISS TESMAN.

And what do you think of it all?

TESMAN.

I'm delighted! Quite delighted! Only I can't think what we are to do with the two empty rooms between this inner parlour and Hedda's bedroom.

MISS TESMAN.

[*Laughing.*] Oh my dear George, I daresay you may find some use for them—in the course of time.

TESMAN.

Why of course you are quite right, Aunt Julia! You mean as my library increases—eh?

MISS TESMAN.

Yes, quite so, my dear boy. It was your library I was thinking of.

TESMAN.

I am specially pleased on Hedda's account. Often and often, before we were engaged, she said that she would never care to live anywhere but in Secretary Falk's villa.[1]

[1] In the original, "Statsrådinde Falks villa"—showing that it had belonged to the widow of a cabinet minister.

MISS TESMAN.

Yes, it was lucky that this very house should come into the market, just after you had started.

TESMAN.

Yes, Aunt Julia, the luck was on our side, wasn't it—eh?

MISS TESMAN.

But the expense, my dear George! You will find it very expensive, all this.

TESMAN.

[*Looks at her, a little cast down.*] Yes, I suppose I shall, Aunt!

MISS TESMAN.

Oh, frightfully!

TESMAN.

How much do you think? In round numbers?—Eh?

MISS TESMAN.

Oh, I can't even guess until all the accounts come in.

TESMAN.

Well, fortunately, Judge Brack has secured the most favourable terms for me,—so he said in a letter to Hedda.

MISS TESMAN.

Yes, don't be uneasy, my dear boy.—Besides, I have given security for the furniture and all the carpets.

TESMAN.

Security? You? My dear Aunt Julia—what sort of security could you give?

MISS TESMAN.

I have given a mortgage on our annuity.

TESMAN.

[*Jumps up.*] What! On your—and Aunt Rina's annuity!

MISS TESMAN.

Yes, I knew of no other plan, you see.

TESMAN.

[*Placing himself before her.*] Have you gone out of your senses, Auntie! Your annuity—it's all that you and Aunt Rina have to live upon.

MISS TESMAN.

Well well—don't get so excited about it. It's only a matter of form you know—Judge Brack assured me of that. It was he that was kind enough to arrange the whole affair for me A mere matter of form, he said.

TESMAN.

Yes, that may be all very well. But nevertheless——

MISS TESMAN.

You will have your own salary to depend upon now. And, good heavens, even if we did have to pay up a little——! To eke things out a bit at the start——! Why, it would be nothing but a pleasure to us.

TESMAN.

Oh Auntie—will you never be tired of making sacrifices for me!

MISS TESMAN.

[*Rises and lays her hand on his shoulders.*] Have

I any other happiness in this world except to smooth your way for you, my dear boy? You, who have had neither father nor mother to depend on. And now we have reached the goal, George! Things have looked black enough for us, sometimes; but, thank heaven, now you have nothing to fear.

TESMAN.

Yes, it is really marvellous how everything has turned out for the best.

MISS TESMAN.

And the people who opposed you—who wanted to bar the way for you—now you have them at your feet. They have fallen, George Your most dangerous rival—his fall was the worst.—And now he has to lie on the bed he has made for himself—poor misguided creature.

TESMAN.

Have you heard anything of Eilert? Since I went away, I mean.

MISS TESMAN.

Only that he is said to have published a new book.

TESMAN.

What! Eilert Lövborg! Recently—eh?

MISS TESMAN.

Yes, so they say. Heaven knows whether it can be worth anything! Ah, when your new book appears—that will be another story, George! What is it to be about?

TESMAN.

It will deal with the domestic industries of Brabant during the Middle Ages.

MISS TESMAN.

Fancy—to be able to write on such a subject as that!

TESMAN.

However, it may be some time before the book is ready. I have all these collections to arrange first, you see.

MISS TESMAN.

Yes, collecting and arranging—no one can beat you at that. There you are my poor brother's own son.

TESMAN.

I am looking forward eagerly to setting to work at it; especially now that I have my own delightful home to work in.

MISS TESMAN.

And, most of all, now that you have got the wife of your heart, my dear George.

TESMAN.

[*Embracing her.*] Oh yes, yes, Aunt Julia Hedda—she is the best part of it all! [*Looks towards the doorway.*] I believe I hear her coming —eh?

HEDDA *enters from the left through the inner room. She is a woman of nine-and-twenty. Her face and figure show refinement and distinction. Her complexion is pale and opaque. Her steel-grey eyes express a cold, unruffled repose. Her hair is of an agreeable medium brown, but not particularly abundant. She is dressed in a tasteful, somewhat loose-fitting morning gown.*

MISS TESMAN.

[*Going to meet* HEDDA.] Good morning, my dear Hedda! Good morning, and a hearty welcome

HEDDA.

[*Holds out her hand.*] Good morning, dear Miss Tesman! So early a call! That is kind of you.

MISS TESMAN.

[*With some embarrassment.*] Well—has the bride slept well in her new home?

HEDDA.

Oh yes, thanks. Passably.

TESMAN.

[*Laughing.*] Passably! Come, that's good, Hedda! You were sleeping like a stone when I got up.

HEDDA.

Fortunately. Of course one has always to accustom one's self to new surroundings, Miss Tesman—little by little. [*Looking towards the left.*] Oh—there the servant has gone and opened the veranda door, and let in a whole flood of sunshine

MISS TESMAN.

[*Going towards the door.*] Well, then we will shut it.

HEDDA.

No no, not that! Tesman, please draw the curtains. That will give a softer light.

TESMAN.

[*At the door.*] All right—all right.—There now, Hedda, now you have both shade and fresh air.

HEDDA.

Yes, fresh air we certainly must have, with all these stacks of flowers——. But—won't you sit down, Miss Tesman?

MISS TESMAN.

No, thank you. Now that I have seen that everything is all right here—thank heaven!—I must be getting home again. My sister is lying longing for me, poor thing.

TESMAN.

Give her my very best love, Auntie; and say I shall look in and see her later in the day.

MISS TESMAN.

Yes, yes, I'll be sure to tell her. But by-the-bye, George—[*Feeling in her dress pocket*]—I had almost forgotten—I have something for you here.

TESMAN.

What is it, Auntie? Eh?

MISS TESMAN.

[*Produces a flat parcel wrapped in newspaper and hands it to him.*] Look here, my dear boy.

TESMAN.

[*Opening the parcel.*] Well, I declare!—Have you

really saved them for me, Aunt Julia! Hedda! isn't this touching—eh?

HEDDA.

[*Beside the whatnot on the right.*] Well, what is it?

TESMAN.

My old morning-shoes! My slippers.

HEDDA.

Indeed. I remember you often spoke of them while we were abroad.

TESMAN.

Yes, I missed them terribly. [*Goes up to her.*] Now you shall see them, Hedda!

HEDDA.

[*Going towards the stove.*] Thanks, I really don't care about it.

TESMAN.

[*Following her.*] Only think—ill as she was, Aunt Rina embroidered these for me. Oh you can't think how many associations cling to them.

HEDDA.

[*At the table.*] Scarcely for me.

MISS TESMAN.

Of course not for Hedda, George.

TESMAN.

Well, but now that she belongs to the family, I thought——

HEDDA.

[*Interrupting.*] We shall never get on with this servant, Tesman.

MISS TESMAN.

Not get on with Berta?

TESMAN.

Why, dear, what puts *that* in your head? Eh?

HEDDA.

[*Pointing.*] Look there! She has left her old bonnet lying about on a chair.

TESMAN.

[*In consternation, drops the slippers on the floor.* Why, Hedda——

HEDDA.

Just fancy, if any one should come in and see it!

TESMAN.

But Hedda—that's Aunt Julia's bonnet.

HEDDA.

Is it!

MISS TESMAN.

[*Taking up the bonnet.*] Yes, indeed it's mine. And, what's more, it's not old, Madam Hedda.

HEDDA.

I really did not look closely at it, Miss Tesman.

MISS TESMAN.

[*Trying on the bonnet.*] Let me tell you it's the first time I have worn it—the very first time.

TESMAN.

And a very nice bonnet it is too—quite a beauty!

MISS TESMAN.

Oh, it's no such great things, George. [*Looks around her.*] My parasol——? Ah, here. [*Takes it.*] For this is mine too—[*mutters*]—not Berta's.

TESMAN.

A new bonnet and a new parasol! Only think, Hedda!

HEDDA.

Very handsome indeed.

TESMAN.

Yes, isn't it? Eh? But Auntie, take a good look at Hedda before you go! See how handsome she is!

MISS TESMAN.

Oh, my dear boy, there's nothing new in that. Hedda was always lovely.

[*She nods and goes towards the right.*

TESMAN.

[*Following.*] Yes, but have you noticed what splendid condition she is in? How she has filled out on the journey?

HEDDA.

[*Crossing the room.*] Oh, do be quiet——!

MISS TESMAN.

[*Who has stopped and turned.*] Filled out?

TESMAN.

Of course you don't notice it so much now that she has that dress on. But I, who can see——

HEDDA.

[*At the glass door, impatiently.*] Oh, you can't see anything.

TESMAN.

It must be the mountain air in the Tyrol——

HEDDA.

[*Curtly, interrupting.*] I am exactly as I was when I started.

TESMAN.

So you insist; but I'm quite certain you are not. Don't you agree with me, Auntie?

MISS TESMAN.

[*Who has been gazing at her with folded hands.*] Hedda is lovely—lovely—lovely. [*Goes up to her, takes her head between both hands, draws it downwards, and kisses her hair.*] God bless and preserve Hedda Tesman—for George's sake.

HEDDA.

[*Gently freeing herself.*] Oh—! Let me go.

MISS TESMAN.

[*In quiet emotion.*] I shall not let a day pass without coming to see you.

TESMAN.

No you won't, will you, Auntie? Eh?

MISS TESMAN.

Good-bye—good-bye!

[*She goes out by the hall door.* TESMAN *accompanies her. The door remains half open.* TESMAN *can be heard repeating his message to Aunt Rina and his thanks for the slippers.*

[*In the meantime,* HEDDA *walks about the room, raising her arms and clenching her hands as if in desperation. Then she flings back the curtains from the glass door, and stands there looking out.*

[*Presently* TESMAN *returns and closes the door behind him.*

TESMAN.

[*Picks up the slippers from the floor.*] What are you looking at, Hedda?

HEDDA.

[*Once more calm and mistress of herself.*] I am only looking at the leaves. They are so yellow—so withered.

TESMAN.

[*Wraps up the slippers and lays them on the table.*] Well you see, we are well into September now.

HEDDA.

[*Again restless.*] Yes, to think of it!—Already in—in September.

TESMAN.

Don't you think Aunt Julia's manner was strange, dear? Almost solemn? Can you imagine what was the matter with her? Eh?

HEDDA.

I scarcely know her, you see. Is she not often like that?

TESMAN.

No, not as she was to-day.

HEDDA.

[*Leaving the glass door.*] Do you think she was annoyed about the bonnet?

TESMAN.

Oh, scarcely at all. Perhaps a little, just at the moment——

HEDDA.

But what an idea, to pitch her bonnet about in the drawing-room! No one does that sort of thing.

TESMAN.

Well you may be sure Aunt Julia won't do it again.

HEDDA.

In any case, I shall manage to make my peace with her.

TESMAN.

Yes, my dear, good Hedda, if you only would.

HEDDA.

When you call this afternoon, you might invite her to spend the evening here.

TESMAN.

Yes, that I will. And there's one thing more you could do that would delight her heart.

HEDDA.

What is it?

TESMAN.

If you could only prevail on yourself to say *du*[1] to her. For my sake, Hedda? Eh?

HEDDA.

No no, Tesman—you really mustn't ask that of me. I have told you so already. I shall try to call her "Aunt"; and you must be satisfied with that.

TESMAN.

Well well. Only I think now that you belong to the family, you——

HEDDA.

H'm—I can't in the least see why——

[*She goes up towards the middle doorway.*

TESMAN.

[*After a pause.*] Is there anything the matter with you, Hedda? Eh?

HEDDA.

I'm only looking at my old piano. It doesn't go at all well with all the other things.

TESMAN.

The first time I draw my salary, we'll see about exchanging it.

HEDDA.

No, no—no exchanging. I don't want to part with it. Suppose we put it there in the inner

[1] *Du* = thou; Tesman means, "If you could persuade yourself to *tutoyer* her."

room, and then get another here in its place. When it's convenient, I mean.

TESMAN.

[*A little taken aback.*] Yes—of course we could do that.

HEDDA.

[*Takes up the bouquet from the piano.*] These flowers were not here last night when we arrived.

TESMAN.

Aunt Julia must have brought them for you.

HEDDA.

[*Examining the bouquet.*] A visiting-card. [*Takes it out and reads:*] "Shall return later in the day." Can you guess whose card it is?

TESMAN.

No. Whose? Eh?

HEDDA.

The name is "Mrs. Elvsted."

TESMAN.

Is it really? Sheriff Elvsted's wife? Miss Rysing that was.

HEDDA.

Exactly. The girl with the irritating hair, that she was always showing off. An old flame of yours I've been told.

TESMAN.

[*Laughing.*] Oh, that didn't last long; and it was before I knew you, Hedda. But fancy her being in town!

HEDDA.

It's odd that she should call upon us. I have scarcely seen her since we left school.

TESMAN.

I haven't seen her either for—heaven knows how long. I wonder how she can endure to live in such an out-of-the way hole—eh?

HEDDA.

[*After a moment's thought, says suddenly.*] Tell me, Tesman—isn't it somewhere near there that he—that—Eilert Lövborg is living?

TESMAN.

Yes, he is somewhere in that part of the country.

BERTA *enters by the hall door.*

BERTA.

That lady, ma'am, that brought some flowers a little while ago, is here again. [*Pointing.*] The flowers you have in your hand, ma'am.

HEDDA.

Ah, is she? Well, please show her in.

BERTA *opens the door for* MRS. ELVSTED, *and goes out herself.*—MRS. ELVSTED *is a woman of fragile figure, with pretty, soft features. Her eyes are light blue, large, round, and somewhat prominent, with a startled, inquiring expression. Her hair is remarkably light, almost flaxen, and unusually abundant and wavy. She is a couple of years younger than* HEDDA. *She wears a dark visiting dress, tasteful, but not quite in the latest fashion.*

HEDDA.

[*Receives her warmly.*] How do you do, my dear Mrs. Elvsted? It's delightful to see you again.

MRS. ELVSTED.

[*Nervously, struggling for self-control.*] Yes, it's a very long time since we met.

TESMAN.

[*Gives her his hand.*] And we too—eh?

HEDDA.

Thanks for your lovely flowers——

MRS. ELVSTED.

Oh, not at all——. I would have come straight here yesterday afternoon; but I heard that you were away——

TESMAN.

Have you just come to town? Eh?

MRS. ELVSTED.

I arrived yesterday, about midday. Oh, I was quite in despair when I heard that you were not at home.

HEDDA.

In despair! How so?

TESMAN.

Why, my dear Mrs. Rysing—I mean Mrs. Elvsted——

HEDDA.

I hope that you are not in any trouble?

MRS. ELVSTED.

Yes, I am. And I don't know another living creature here that I can turn to.

HEDDA.

[*Laying the bouquet on the table.*] Come—let us sit here on the sofa——

MRS. ELVSTED.

Oh, I am too restless to sit down.

HEDDA.

Oh no, you're not. Come here.

[*She draws* MRS. ELVSTED *down upon the sofa and sits at her side.*

TESMAN.

Well? What is it, Mrs. Elvsted——?

HEDDA.

Has anything particular happened to you at home?

MRS. ELVSTED.

Yes—and no. Oh—I am so anxious you should not misunderstand me——

HEDDA.

Then your best plan is to tell us the whole story, Mrs. Elvsted.

TESMAN.

I suppose that's what you have come for—eh?

MRS. ELVSTED.

Yes, yes—of course it is. Well then, I must

tell you—if you don't already know—that Eilert Lövborg is in town, too.

HEDDA.

Lövborg——!

TESMAN.

What! Has Eilert Lövborg come back? Fancy that, Hedda!

HEDDA.

Well well—I hear it.

MRS. ELVSTED.

He has been here a week already. Just fancy —a whole week! In this terrible town, alone! With so many temptations on all sides.

HEDDA.

But, my dear Mrs. Elvsted—how does *he* concern you so much?

MRS. ELVSTED.

[*Looks at her with a startled air, and says rapidly.*] He was the children's tutor.

HEDDA.

Your children's?

MRS. ELVSTED.

My husband's. I have none.

HEDDA.

Your step-children's, then?

MRS. ELVSTED.

Yes.

TESMAN.

[*Somewhat hesitatingly.*] Then was he—I don't know how to express it—was he—regular enough in his habits to be fit for the post? Eh?

MRS. ELVSTED.

For the last two years his conduct has been irreproachable.

TESMAN.

Has it indeed? Fancy that, Hedda!

HEDDA.

I hear it.

MRS. ELVSTED.

Perfectly irreproachable, I assure you! In every respect. But all the same—now that I know he is here—in this great town—and with a large sum of money in his hands—I can't help being in mortal fear for him.

TESMAN.

Why did he not remain where he was? With you and your husband? Eh?

MRS. ELVSTED.

After his book was published he was too restless and unsettled to remain with us.

TESMAN.

Yes, by-the-bye, Aunt Julia told me he had published a new book.

MRS. ELVSTED.

Yes, a big book, dealing with the march of civilisation—in broad outline, as it were. It came out about a fortnight ago. And since it has sold so well, and been so much read—and made such a sensation——

TESMAN.

Has it indeed? It must be something he has had lying by since his better days.

MRS. ELVSTED.

Long ago, you mean?

TESMAN.

Yes.

MRS. ELVSTED.

No, he has written it all since he has been with us—within the last year.

TESMAN.

Isn't that good news, Hedda? Think of that.

MRS. ELVSTED.

Ah yes, if only it would last!

HEDDA.

Have you seen him here in town?

MRS. ELVSTED.

No, not yet. I have had the greatest difficulty in finding out his address. But this morning I discovered it at last.

HEDDA.

[*Looks searchingly at her.*] Do you know, it seems to me a little odd of your husband—h'm——

MRS. ELVSTED.

[*Starting nervously.*] Of my husband! What?

HEDDA.

That he should send you to town on such an errand—that he does not come himself and look after his friend.

MRS. ELVSTED.

Oh no, no—my husband has no time. And besides, I—I had some shopping to do.

HEDDA.

[*With a slight smile.*] Ah, that is a different matter.

MRS. ELVSTED.

[*Rising quickly and uneasily.*] And now I beg and implore you, Mr. Tesman—receive Eilert Lövborg kindly if he comes to you! And that he is sure to do. You see you were such great friends in the old days. And then you are interested in the same studies—the same branch of science—so far as I can understand.

TESMAN.

We used to be, at any rate.

MRS. ELVSTED.

That is why I beg so earnestly that you—you too—will keep a sharp eye upon him. Oh, you will promise me that, Mr. Tesman—won't you?

TESMAN.

With the greatest of pleasure, Mrs. Rysing——

HEDDA.

Elvsted.

TESMAN.

I assure you I shall do all I possibly can for Eilert. You may rely upon me.

MRS. ELVSTED.

Oh, how very, very kind of you! [*Presses his hands.*] Thanks, thanks, thanks! [*Frightened.*] You see, my husband is so very fond of him!

HEDDA.

[*Rising.*] You ought to write to him, Tesman. Perhaps he may not care to come to you of his own accord.

TESMAN.

Well, perhaps it would be the right thing to do, Hedda? Eh?

HEDDA.

And the sooner the better. Why not at once?

MRS. ELVSTED.

[*Imploringly.*] Oh, if you only would!

TESMAN.

I'll write this moment. Have you his address, Mrs.—Mrs. Elvsted.

MRS. ELVSTED.

Yes. [*Takes a slip of paper from her pocket, and hands it to him.*] Here it is.

TESMAN.

Good, good. Then I'll go in—— [*Looks about him.*] By-the-bye,—my slippers? Oh, here.

[*Takes the packet, and is about to go.*

HEDDA.

Be sure you write him a cordial, friendly letter. And a good long one too.

TESMAN.

Yes, I will.

MRS. ELVSTED.

But please, please don't say a word to show that I have suggested it.

TESMAN.

No, how could you think I would? Eh?

[*He goes out to the right, through the inner room.*

HEDDA.

[*Goes up to* MRS. ELVSTED, *smiles, and says in a low voice.*] There! We have killed two birds with one stone.

MRS. ELVSTED.

What do you mean?

HEDDA.

Could you not see that I wanted him to go?

MRS. ELVSTED.

Yes, to write the letter——

HEDDA.

And that I might speak to you alone.

MRS. ELVSTED.

[*Confused.*] About the same thing?

HEDDA.

Precisely.

MRS. ELVSTED.

[*Apprehensively.*] But there is nothing more Mrs. Tesman! Absolutely nothing!

HEDDA.

Oh yes, but there is. There is a great deal more—I can see that. Sit here—and we'll have a cosy, confidential chat.

[*She forces* MRS. ELVSTED *to sit in the easy-chair beside the stove, and seats herself on one of the footstools.*

MRS. ELVSTED.

[*Anxiously, looking at her watch.*] But, my dear Mrs. Tesman—I was really on the point of going.

HEDDA.

Oh, you can't be in such a hurry.—Well? Now tell me something about your life at home.

MRS. ELVSTED.

Oh, that is just what I care least to speak about.

HEDDA.

But to me, dear——? Why, weren't we schoolfellows?

MRS. ELVSTED.

Yes, but you were in the class above me. Oh, how dreadfully afraid of you I was then!

HEDDA.

Afraid of me?

MRS. ELVSTED.

Yes, dreadfully. For when we met on the stairs you used always to pull my hair.

HEDDA.

Did I, really?

MRS. ELVSTED.

Yes, and once you said you would burn it off my head.

HEDDA.

Oh that was all nonsense, of course.

MRS. ELVSTED.

Yes, but I was so silly in those days.—And since then, too—we have drifted so far—far apart from each other. Our circles have been so entirely different.

HEDDA.

Well then, we must try to drift together again. Now listen! At school we said *du*[1] to each other; and we called each other by our Christian names——

MRS. ELVSTED.

No, I am sure you must be mistaken.

HEDDA.

No, not at all! I can remember quite distinctly. So now we are going to renew our old friendship. [*Draws the footstool closer to* MRS. ELVSTED.] There now! [*Kisses her cheek.*] You must say *du* to me and call me Hedda.

MRS. ELVSTED.

[*Presses and pats her hands.*] Oh, how good and kind you are! I am not used to such kindness.

HEDDA.

There, there, there! And I shall say *du* to you, as in the old days, and call you my dear Thora.

[1] See footnote, p. 27.

MRS. ELVSTED.

My name is Thea.[1]

HEDDA.

Why, of course! I meant Thea. [*Looks at her compassionately.*] So you are not accustomed to goodness and kindness, Thea? Not in your own home?

MRS. ELVSTED.

Oh, if I only had a home! But I haven't any; I have never had a home.

HEDDA.

[*Looks at her for a moment.*] I almost suspected as much.

MRS. ELVSTED.

[*Gazing helplessly before her.*] Yes—yes—yes.

HEDDA.

I don't quite remember—was it not as housekeeper that you first went to Mr. Elvsted's?

MRS. ELVSTED.

I really went as governess. But his wife—his late wife—was an invalid,—and rarely left her room. So I had to look after the housekeeping as well.

HEDDA.

And then—at last—you became mistress of the house.

MRS. ELVSTED.

[*Sadly.*] Yes, I did.

HEDDA.

Let me see—about how long ago was that?

[1] Pronounce *Tora* and *Taya*.

MRS. ELVSTED.

My marriage?

HEDDA.

Yes.

MRS. ELVSTED.

Five years ago.

HEDDA.

To be sure; it must be that.

MRS. ELVSTED.

Oh those five years——! Or at all events the last two or three of them! Oh, if you[1] could only imagine——

HEDDA.

[*Giving her a little slap on the hand.*] *De*? Fie, Thea!

MRS. ELVSTED.

Yes, yes, I will try—— Well, if—you could only imagine and understand——

HEDDA.

[*Lightly.*] Eilert Lövborg has been in your neighbourhood about three years, hasn't he?

MRS. ELVSTED.

[*Looks at her doubtfully.*] Eilert Lövborg? Yes—he has.

HEDDA.

Had you known him before, in town here?

MRS. ELVSTED.

Scarcely at all. I mean—I knew him by name of course.

[1] Mrs. Elvsted here uses the formal pronoun *De*, whereupon Hedda rebukes her. In her next speech Mrs. Elvsted says *du*.

HEDDA.

But you saw a good deal of him in the country?

MRS. ELVSTED.

Yes, he came to us every day. You see, he gave the children lessons; for in the long run I couldn't manage it all myself.

HEDDA.

No, that's clear.—And your husband——? I suppose he is often away from home?

MRS. ELVSTED.

Yes. Being sheriff, you know, he has to travel about a good deal in his district.

HEDDA.

[*Leaning against the arm of the chair.*] Thea—my poor, sweet Thea—now you must tell me everything—exactly as it stands.

MRS. ELVSTED.

Well then, you must question me.

HEDDA.

What sort of a man is your husband, Thea? I mean—you know—in everyday life. Is he kind to you?

MRS. ELVSTED.

[*Evasively.*] I am sure he means well in everything.

HEDDA.

I should think he must be altogether too old for you. There is at least twenty years' difference between you, is there not?

MRS. ELVSTED.

[*Irritably.*] Yes, that is true, too. Everything about him is repellent to me! We have not a thought in common. We have no single point of sympathy—he and I.

HEDDA.

But is he not fond of you all the same? In his own way?

MRS. ELVSTED.

Oh I really don't know. I think he regards me simply as a useful property. And then it doesn't cost much to keep me. I am not expensive.

HEDDA.

That is stupid of you.

MRS. ELVSTED.

[*Shakes her head.*] It cannot be otherwise—not with him. I don't think he really cares for any one but himself—and perhaps a little for the children.

HEDDA

And for Eilert Lövberg, Thea.

MRS. ELVSTED.

[*Looking at her.*] For Eilert Lövborg? What puts that into your head?

HEDDA.

Well, my dear—I should say, when he sends you after him all the way to town—— [*Smiling almost imperceptibly.*] And besides, you said so yourself, to Tesman.

MRS. ELVSTED.

[*With a little nervous twitch.*] Did I? Yes, I suppose I did. [*Vehemently, but not loudly.*] No—I may just as well make a clean breast of it at once! For it must all come out in any case.

HEDDA.

Why, my dear Thea——?

MRS. ELVSTED.

Well, to make a long story short: My husband did not know that I was coming.

HEDDA.

What! Your husband didn't know it!

MRS. ELVSTED.

No, of course not. For that matter, he was away from home himself—he was travelling. Oh, I could bear it no longer, Hedda! I couldn't indeed—so utterly alone as I should have been in future.

HEDDA.

Well? And then?

MRS. ELVSTED.

So I put together some of my things—what I needed most—as quietly as possible. And then I left the house.

HEDDA.

Without a word?

MRS. ELVSTED.

Yes—and took the train straight to town.

HEDDA.

Why, my dear, good Thea—to think of you daring to do it!

MRS. ELVSTED.

[*Rises and moves about the room.*] What else could I possibly do?

HEDDA.

But what do you think your husband will say when you go home again?

MRS. ELVSTED.

[*At the table, looks at her.*] Back to him?

HEDDA.

Of course.

MRS. ELVSTED.

I shall never go back to him again.

HEDDA.

[*Rising and going towards her.*] Then you have left your home—for good and all?

MRS. ELVSTED.

Yes. There was nothing else to be done.

HEDDA.

But then—to take flight so openly

MRS. ELVSTED.

Oh, it's impossible to keep things of that sort secret.

HEDDA.

But what do you think people will say of you, Thea?

MRS. ELVSTED.

They may say what they like, for aught *I* care. [*Seats herself wearily and sadly on the sofa.*] I have done nothing but what I had to do.

HEDDA.

[*After a short silence.*] And what are your plans now? What do you think of doing?

MRS. ELVSTED.

I don't know yet. I only know this, that I must live here, where Eilert Lövborg is—if I am to live at all.

HEDDA.

[*Takes a chair from the table, seats herself beside her, and strokes her hands.*] My dear Thea—how did this—this friendship—between you and Eilert Lövborg come about?

MRS. ELVSTED.

Oh it grew up gradually. I gained a sort of influence over him.

HEDDA.

Indeed?

MRS. ELVSTED.

He gave up his old habits. Not because I asked him to, for I never dared do that. But of course he saw how repulsive they were to me; and so he dropped them.

HEDDA.

[*Concealing an involuntary smile of scorn.*] Then you have reclaimed him—as the saying goes—my little Thea.

MRS. ELVSTED.

So he says himself, at any rate. And he, on his side, has made a real human being of me—taught me to think, and to understand so many things.

HEDDA.

Did he give you lessons too, then?

MRS. ELVSTED.

No, not exactly lessons. But he talked to me—talked about such an infinity of things. And then came the lovely, happy time when I began to share in his work—when he allowed me to help him!

HEDDA.

Oh he did, did he?

MRS. ELVSTED.

Yes! He never wrote anything without my assistance.

HEDDA.

You were two good comrades, in fact?

MRS. ELVSTED.

[*Eagerly.*] Comrades! Yes, fancy, Hedda—that is the very word he used!—Oh, I ought to feel perfectly happy; and yet I cannot; for I don't know how long it will last.

HEDDA.

Are you no surer of him than that?

MRS. ELVSTED.

[*Gloomily.*] A woman's shadow stands between Eilert Lövberg and me.

HEDDA.

[*Looks at her anxiously.*] Who can that be?

MRS. ELVSTED.

I don't know. Some one he knew in his—in his past. Some one he has never been able wholly to forget.

HEDDA.

What has he told you—about this?

MRS. ELVSTED.

He has only once—quite vaguely—alluded to it.

HEDDA.

Well! And what did he say?

MRS. ELVSTED.

He said that when they parted, she threatened to shoot him with a pistol.

HEDDA.

[*With cold composure.*] Oh nonsense! No one does that sort of thing here.

MRS. ELVSTED.

No. And that is why I think it must have been that red-haired singing-woman whom he once——

HEDDA.

Yes, very likely.

MRS. ELVSTED.

For I remember they used to say of her that she carried loaded firearms.

HEDDA.

Oh—then of course it must have been she.

MRS. ELVSTED.

[*Wringing her hands.*] And now just fancy, Hedda—I hear that this singing-woman—that she is in town again! Oh, I don't know what to do——

HEDDA.

[*Glancing towards the inner room.*] Hush! Here comes Tesman. [*Rises and whispers.*] Thea—all this must remain between you and me.

MRS. ELVSTED.

[*Springing up.*] Oh yes—yes! For heaven's sake——!

GEORGE TESMAN, *with a letter in his hand, comes from the right through the inner room.*

TESMAN.

There now—the epistle is finished.

HEDDA.

That's right. And now Mrs. Elvsted is just going. Wait a moment—I'll go with you to the garden gate.

TESMAN.

Do you think Berta could post the letter, Hedda dear?

HEDDA.

[*Takes it.*] I will tell her to.

BERTA *enters from the hall.*

BERTA.

Judge Brack wishes to know if Mrs. Tesman will receive him.

HEDDA.

Yes, ask Judge Brack to come in. And look here—put this letter in the post.

BERTA.

[*Taking the letter.*] Yes, ma'am.

[*She opens the door for* JUDGE BRACK *and goes out herself.* BRACK *is a man of forty-five; thick set, but well-built and elastic in his movements. His face is roundish with an aristocratic profile. His hair is short, still almost black, and carefully dressed. His eyes are lively and sparkling. His eyebrows thick. His moustaches are also thick, with short-cut ends. He wears a well-cut walking-suit, a little too youthful for his age. He uses an eye-glass, which he now and then lets drop.*

JUDGE BRACK.

[*With his hat in his hand, bowing.*] May one venture to call so early in the day?

HEDDA.

Of course one may.

TESMAN.

[*Presses his hand.*] You are welcome at any time. [*Introducing him.*] Judge Brack—Miss Rysing——

HEDDA.

Oh——!

BRACK.

[*Bowing.*] Ah—delighted——

HEDDA.

[*Looks at him and laughs.*] It's nice to have a look at you by daylight, Judge!

BRACK.

Do you find me—altered?

HEDDA.

A little younger, I think.

BRACK.

Thank you so much.

TESMAN.

But what do you think of Hedda—eh? Doesn't she look flourishing? She has actually——

HEDDA.

Oh, do leave me alone. You haven't thanked Judge Brack for all the trouble he has taken——

BRACK.

Oh, nonsense—it was a pleasure to me——

HEDDA.

Yes, you are a friend indeed. But here stands Thea all impatience to be off—so *au revoir* Judge. I shall be back again presently.

[*Mutual salutations.* MRS. ELVSTED *and* HEDDA *go out by the hall door.*

BRACK.

Well,—is your wife tolerably satisfied——

TESMAN.

Yes, we can't thank you sufficiently. Of course she talks of a little re-arrangement here and there; and one or two things are still wanting, We shall have to buy some additional trifles.

BRACK.

Indeed!

TESMAN.

But we won't trouble you about these things. Hedda says she herself will look after what is wanting.—Shan't we sit down? Eh?

BRACK.

Thanks, for a moment. [*Seats himself beside the table.*] There is something I wanted to speak to you about, my dear Tesman.

TESMAN.

Indeed? Ah, I understand! [*Seating himself.*] I suppose it's the serious part of the frolic that is coming now. Eh?

BRACK.

Oh, the money question is not so very pressing; though, for that matter, I wish we had gone a little more economically to work.

TESMAN.

But that would never have done, you know! Think of Hedda, my dear fellow! You, who know her so well——. I couldn't possibly ask her to put up with a shabby style of living!

BRACK.

No, no—that is just the difficulty.

TESMAN.

And then—fortunately—it can't be long before I receive my appointment.

BRACK.

Well, you see—such things are often apt to hang fire for a time.

TESMAN.

Have you heard anything definite? Eh?

BRACK.

Nothing exactly definite——. [*Interrupting himself.*] But by-the-bye—I have one piece of news for you.

TESMAN.

Well?

BRACK.

Your old friend, Eilert Lövborg, has returned to town.

TESMAN.

I know that already.

BRACK.

Indeed! How did you learn it?

TESMAN.

From that lady who went out with Hedda.

BRACK.

Really? What was her name? I didn't quite catch it.

TESMAN.

Mrs. Elvsted.

BRACK.

Aha—Sheriff Elvsted's wife? Of course—he has been living up in their regions.

TESMAN.

And fancy—I'm delighted to hear that he is quite a reformed character!

BRACK.

So they say.

TESMAN.

And then he has published a new book—eh?

BRACK.

Yes, indeed he has.

TESMAN.

And I hear it has made some sensation!

BRACK.

Quite an unusual sensation.

TESMAN.

Fancy—isn't that good news! A man of such extraordinary talents——. I felt so grieved to think that he had gone irretrievably to ruin.

BRACK.

That was what everybody thought.

TESMAN.

But I cannot imagine what he will take to now! How in the world will he be able to make his living? Eh?

[*During the last words,* HEDDA *has entered by the hall door.*

HEDDA.

[*To* BRACK, *laughing with a touch of scorn.*] Tesman is for ever worrying about how people are to make their living.

TESMAN.

Well you see, dear—we were talking about poor Eilert Lövborg.

HEDDA.

[*Glancing at him rapidly.*] Oh, indeed? [*Seats herself in the arm-chair beside the stove and asks indifferently:*] What is the matter with him?

TESMAN.

Well—no doubt he has run through all his property long ago; and he can scarcely write a new book every year—eh? So I really can't see what is to become of him.

BRACK.

Perhaps I can give you some information on that point.

TESMAN.

Indeed!

BRACK.

You must remember that his relations have a ood deal of influence.

TESMAN.

Oh, his relations, unfortunately, have entirely washed their hands of him.

BRACK.

At one time they called him the hope of the family.

TESMAN.

At one time, yes! But he has put an end to all that.

HEDDA.

Who knows? [*With a slight smile.*] I hear they have reclaimed him up at Sheriff Elvsted's——

BRACK.

And then this book that he has published——

TESMAN.

Well well, I hope to goodness they may find something for him to do. I have just written to him. I asked him to come and see us this evening, Hedda dear.

BRACK.

But my dear fellow, you are booked for my bachelors' party this evening. You promised on the pier last night.

HEDDA.

Had you forgotten, Tesman?

TESMAN.

Yes, I had utterly forgotten.

BRACK.

But it doesn't matter, for you may be sure he won't come.

TESMAN

What makes you think that? Eh?

BRACK.

[*With a little hesitation, rising and resting his hands on the back of his chair.*] My dear Tesman — and you too, Mrs. Tesman — I think I ought not to keep you in the dark about something that—that——

TESMAN.

That concerns Eilert——?

BRACK.

Both you and him.

TESMAN.

Well, my dear Judge, out with it.

BRACK.

You must be prepared to find your appointment deferred longer than you desired or expected.

TESMAN.

[*Jumping up uneasily.*] Is there some hitch about it? Eh?

BRACK.

The nomination may perhaps be made conditional on the result of a competition——

TESMAN.

Competition! Think of that, Hedda!

HEDDA.

[*Leans further back in the chair.*] Aha—aha!

TESMAN.

But who can my competitor be? Surely not——?

BRACK.

Yes, precisely—Eilert Lövborg.

TESMAN.

[*Clasping his hands.*] No, no—it's quite inconceivable! Quite impossible! Eh?

BRACK.

H'm—that is what it may come to, all the same.

TESMAN.

Well but, Judge Brack—it would show the most incredible lack of consideration for me. [*Gesticulates with his arms.*] For—just think—I'm a married man! We have married on the strength of these prospects, Hedda and I; and run deep into debt; and borrowed money from Aunt Julia too. Good heavens, they had as good as promised me the appointment. Eh?

BRACK.

Well, well, well—no doubt you will get it in the end; only after a contest.

HEDDA.

[*Immovable in her arm-chair.*] Fancy, Tesman, there will be a sort of sporting interest in that.

TESMAN.

Why, my dearest Hedda, how can you be so indifferent about it.

HEDDA.

[*As before.*] I am not at all indifferent. I am most eager to see who wins.

BRACK.

In any case, Mrs. Tesman, it is best that you should know how matters stand. I mean—before you set about the little purchases I hear you are threatening.

HEDDA.

This can make no difference.

BRACK.

Indeed! Then I have no more to say. Good-bye! [*To* TESMAN.] I shall look in on my way back from my afternoon walk, and take you home with me.

TESMAN.

Oh yes, yes—your news has quite upset me.

HEDDA.

[*Reclining, holds out her hand.*] Good-bye, Judge; and be sure you call in the afternoon.

BRACK.

Many thanks. Good-bye, good-bye!

TESMAN.

[*Accompanying him to the door.*] Good-bye my dear Judge! You must really excuse me——

[JUDGE BRACK *goes out by the hall door.*

TESMAN.

[*Crosses the room.*] Oh Hedda—one should never rush into adventures. Eh?

HEDDA.

[*Looks at him, smiling.*] Do you do that?

TESMAN.

Yes, dear—there is no denying—it was adventurous to go and marry and set up house upon mere expectations.

HEDDA.

Perhaps you are right there.

TESMAN.

Well—at all events, we have our delightful home, Hedda! Fancy, the home we both dreamed of—the home we were in love with, I may almost say. Eh?

HEDDA.

[*Rising slowly and wearily.*] It was part of our compact that we were to go into society—to keep open house.

TESMAN.

Yes, if you only knew how I had been looking forward to it! Fancy—to see you as hostess—in a select circle! Eh? Well, well, well—for the present we shall have to get on without society, Hedda—only to invite Aunt Julia now and then.—Oh, I intended you to lead such an utterly different life, dear——!

HEDDA.

Of course I cannot have my man in livery just yet.

TESMAN.

Oh no, unfortunately. It would be out of the question for us to keep a footman, you know.

HEDDA.

And the saddle-horse I was to have had——

TESMAN.

[*Aghast.*] The saddle-horse!

HEDDA.

——I suppose I must not think of that now.

TESMAN.

Good heavens, no!—that's as clear as daylight

HEDDA.

[*Goes up the room.*] Well, I shall have one thing at least to kill time with in the meanwhile.

TESMAN.

[*Beaming.*] Oh thank heaven for that! What is it, Hedda? Eh?

HEDDA.

[*In the middle doorway, looks at him with covert scorn.*] My pistols, George.

TESMAN.

[*In alarm.*] Your pistols!

HEDDA.

[*With cold eyes.*] General Gabler's pistols.

[*She goes out through the inner room, to the left.*

TESMAN.

[*Rushes up to the middle doorway and calls after her:*] No, for heaven's sake, Hedda darling—don't touch those dangerous things! For my sake, Hedda! Eh?

ACT SECOND

The room at the TESMANS' *as in the first Act, except that the piano has been removed, and an elegant little writing-table with book-shelves put in its place. A smaller table stands near the sofa on the left. Most of the bouquets have been taken away.* MRS. ELVSTED'S *bouquet is upon the large table in front.—It is afternoon.*

HEDDA, *dressed to receive callers, is alone in the room. She stands by the open glass door, loading a revolver. The fellow to it lies in an open pistol-case on the writing-table.*

HEDDA.

[*Looks down the garden, and calls :*] So you are here again, Judge!

BRACK.

[*Is heard calling from a distance.*] As you see, Mrs. Tesman!

HEDDA.

[*Raises the pistol and points.*] Now I'll shoot you, Judge Brack!

BRACK.

[*Calling unseen.*] No, no, no! Don't stand aiming at me!

HEDDA.

This is what comes of sneaking in by the back way.[1] [*She fires.*

[1] "Bagveje" means both "back ways" and "underhand courses."

BRACK.

[*Nearer.*] Are you out of your senses——!

HEDDA.

Dear me—did I happen to hit you?

BRACK.

[*Still outside.*] I wish you would let these pranks alone!

HEDDA.

Come in then, Judge.

JUDGE BRACK, *dressed as though for a men's party, enters by the glass door. He carries a light overcoat over his arm.*

BRACK.

What the deuce—haven't you tired of that sport, yet? What are you shooting at?

HEDDA.

Oh, I am only firing in the air.

BRACK.

[*Gently takes the pistol out of her hand.*] Allow me, madam! [*Looks at it.*] Ah—I know this pistol well! [*Looks around.*] Where is the case? Ah, here it is. [*Lays the pistol in it, and shuts it.*] Now we won't play at that game any more to-day.

HEDDA.

Then what in heaven's name would you have me do with myself?

BRACK.

Have you had no visitors?

HEDDA.

[*Closing the glass door.*] Not one. I suppose all our set are still out of town.

BRACK.

And is Tesman not at home either?

HEDDA.

[*At the writing-table, putting the pistol-case in a drawer which she shuts.*] No. He rushed off to his aunt's directly after lunch; he didn't expect you so early.

BRACK.

H'm—how stupid of me not to have thought of that!

HEDDA.

[*Turning her head to look at him.*] Why stupid?

BRACK.

Because if I had thought of it I should have come a little—earlier.

HEDDA.

[*Crossing the room.*] Then you would have found no one to receive you; for I have been in my room changing my dress ever since lunch.

BRACK.

And is there no sort of little chink that we could hold a parley through?

HEDDA.

You have forgotten to arrange one.

BRACK.

That was another piece of stupidity.

HEDDA.

Well, we must just settle down here—and wait. Tesman is not likely to be back for some time yet.

BRACK.

Never mind; I shall not be impatient.

HEDDA *seats herself in the corner of the sofa.* BRACK *lays his overcoat over the back of the nearest chair, and sits down, but keeps his hat in his hand. A short silence. They look at each other.*

HEDDA.

Well?

BRACK.

[*In the same tone.*] Well?

HEDDA

I spoke first.

BRACK.

[*Bending a little forward.*] Come, let us have a cosy little chat, Mrs. Hedda.[1]

HEDDA.

[*Leaning further back in the sofa.*] Does it not seem like a whole eternity since our last talk? Of course I don't count those few words yesterday evening and this morning.

BRACK.

You mean since our last confidential talk? Our last *tête-à-tête?*

[1] As this form of address is contrary to English usage, and as the note of familiarity would be lacking in "Mrs. Tesman," Brack may, in stage representation, say "Miss Hedda," thus ignoring her marriage and reverting to the form of address no doubt customary between them of old.

HEDDA.

Well yes—since you put it so.

BRACK.

Not a day has passed but I have wished that you were home again.

HEDDA.

And I have done nothing but wish the same thing.

BRACK.

You? Really, Mrs. Hedda? And I thought you had been enjoying your tour so much!

HEDDA.

Oh yes, you may be sure of that!

BRACK.

But Tesman's letters spoke of nothing but happiness.

HEDDA.

Oh, Tesman! You see, he thinks nothing so delightful as grubbing in libraries and making copies of old parchments, or whatever you call them.

BRACK.

[*With a spice of malice.*] Well, that is his vocation in life—or part of it at any rate.

HEDDA.

Yes, of course; and no doubt when it's your vocation——. But *I!* Oh, my dear Mr. Brack, how mortally bored I have been.

BRACK.

[*Sympathetically.*] Do you really say so? In downright earnest?

HEDDA

Yes, you can surely understand it——! To go for six whole months without meeting a soul that knew anything of our circle, or could talk about the things we are interested in.

BRACK.

Yes, yes—I too should feel that a deprivation.

HEDDA.

And then, what I found most intolerable of all——

BRACK.

Well?

HEDDA.

——was being everlastingly in the company of—one and the same person——

BRACK.

[*With a nod of assent.*] Morning, noon, and night, yes—at all possible times and seasons.

HEDDA.

I said "everlastingly."

BRACK.

Just so. But I should have thought, with our excellent Tesman, one could——

HEDDA.

Tesman is—a specialist, my dear Judge.

BRACK.

Undeniably.

HEDDA.

And specialists are not at all amusing to travel with. Not in the long run at any rate.

BRACK.

Not even—the specialist one happens to love?

HEDDA.

Faugh—don't use that sickening word!

BRACK.

[*Taken aback.*] What do you say, Mrs. Hedda?

HEDDA.

[*Half laughing, half irritated.*] You should just try it! To hear of nothing but the history of civilisation, morning, noon, and night——

BRACK.

Everlastingly.

HEDDA.

Yes yes yes! And then all this about the domestic industry of the middle ages——! That's the most disgusting part of it!

BRACK.

[*Looks searchingly at her.*] But tell me—in that case, how am I to understand your——? H'm——

HEDDA.

My accepting George Tesman, you mean?

BRACK.

Well, let us put it so.

HEDDA.

Good heavens, do you see anything so wonderful in that?

BRACK.

Yes and no—Mrs. Hedda.

HEDDA.

I had positively danced myself tired, my dear Judge. My day was done—— [*With a slight shudder.*] Oh no—I won't say that; nor think it either!

BRACK.

You have assuredly no reason to.

HEDDA.

Oh, reasons—— [*Watching him closely.*] And George Tesman—after all, you must admit that he is correctness itself.

BRACK.

His correctness and respectability are beyond all question.

HEDDA.

And I don't see anything absolutely ridiculous about him.—Do you?

BRACK.

Ridiculous? N—no—I shouldn't exactly say so——

HEDDA.

Well—and his powers of research, at all events, are untiring.—I see no reason why he should not one day come to the front, after all.

BRACK.

[*Looks at her hesitatingly.*] I thought that you, like

every one else, expected him to attain the highest distinction.

HEDDA.

[*With an expression of fatigue.*] Yes, so I did. —And then, since he was bent, at all hazards, on being allowed to provide for me—I really don't know why I should not have accepted his offer?

BRACK.

No—if you look at it in that light——

HEDDA.

It was more than my other adorers were prepared to do for me, my dear Judge.

BRACK.

[*Laughing.*] Well, I can't answer for all the rest; but as for myself, you know quite well that I have always entertained a—a certain respect for the marriage tie—for marriage as an institution, Mrs. Hedda.

HEDDA.

[*Jestingly.*] Oh, I assure you I have never cherished any hopes with respect to you.

BRACK.

All I require is a pleasant and intimate interior, where I can make myself useful in every way, and am free to come and go as—as a trusted friend——

HEDDA.

Of the master of the house, do you mean?

BRACK.

[*Bowing.*] Frankly—of the mistress first of all; but of course of the master too, in the second place. Such a triangular friendship—if I may call it so—is really a great convenience for all parties, let me tell you.

HEDDA.

Yes, I have many a time longed for some one to make a third on our travels. Oh—those railway-carriage *tête-à-têtes*——!

BRACK.

Fortunately your wedding journey is over now.

HEDDA.

[*Shaking her head.*] Not by a long—long way. I have only arrived at a station on the line.

BRACK.

Well, then the passengers jump out and move about a little, Mrs. Hedda.

HEDDA.

I never jump out.

BRACK.

Really?

HEDDA.

No—because there is always some one standing by to——

BRACK.

[*Laughing.*] To look at your ankles, do you mean?

HEDDA.

Precisely.

BRACK.

Well but, dear me——

HEDDA.

[*With a gesture of repulsion.*] I won't have it.

I would rather keep my seat where I happen to be —and continue the *tête-à-tête.*

BRACK.

But suppose a third person were to jump in and join the couple.

HEDDA.

Ah—that is quite another matter!

BRACK.

A trusted, sympathetic friend——

HEDDA.

——with a fund of conversation on all sorts of lively topics——

BRACK.

——and not the least bit of a specialist!

HEDDA.

[*With an audible sigh.*] Yes, that would be a relief indeed.

BRACK.

[*Hears the front door open, and glances in that direction.*] The triangle is completed.

HEDDA.

[*Half aloud.*] And on goes the train.

GEORGE TESMAN, *in a grey walking-suit, with a soft felt hat, enters from the hall. He has a number of unbound books under his arm and in his pockets.*

TESMAN.

[*Goes up to the table beside the corner settee.*] Ouf—what a load for a warm day—all these books.

[*Lays them on the table.*] I'm positively perspiring, Hedda. Hallo—are you there already, my dear Judge? Eh? Berta didn't tell me.

BRACK.

[*Rising.*] I came in through the garden.

HEDDA.

What books have you got there?

TESMAN.

[*Stands looking them through.*] Some new books on my special subjects—quite indispensable to me.

HEDDA.

Your special subjects?

BRACK.

Yes, books on his special subjects, Mrs. Tesman.

[BRACK *and* HEDDA *exchange a confidential smile.*

HEDDA.

Do you need still more books on your special subjects?

TESMAN.

Yes, my dear Hedda, one can never have too many of them. Of course one must keep up with all that is written and published.

HEDDA.

Yes, I suppose one must.

TESMAN.

[*Searching among his books.*] And look here—I have got hold of Eilert Lövborg's new book too.

[*Offering it to her.*] Perhaps you would like to glance through it, Hedda? Eh?

HEDDA.

No, thank you. Or rather—afterwards perhaps.

TESMAN.

I looked into it a little on the way home.

BRACK.

Well, what do you think of it—as a specialist?

TESMAN.

I think it shows quite remarkable soundness of judgment. He never wrote like that before. [*Putting the books together.*] Now I shall take all these into my study. I'm longing to cut the leaves——! And then I must change my clothes. [*To* BRACK.] I suppose we needn't start just yet? Eh?

BRACK.

Oh, dear no—there is not the slightest hurry.

TESMAN.

Well then, I will take my time. [*Is going with his books, but stops in the doorway and turns.*] By-the-bye, Hedda—Aunt Julia is not coming this evening.

HEDDA.

Not coming? Is it that affair of the bonnet that keeps her away?

TESMAN.

Oh, not at all. How could you think such a thing of Aunt Julia? Just fancy——! The fact is, Aunt Rina is very ill.

HEDDA.

She always is.

TESMAN.

Yes, but to-day she is much worse than usual, poor dear.

HEDDA.

Oh, then it's only natural that her sister should remain with her. I must bear my disappointment.

TESMAN,

And you can't imagine, dear, how delighted Aunt Julia seemed to be—because you had come home looking so flourishing!

HEDDA.

[*Half aloud, rising.*] Oh, those everlasting Aunts!

TESMAN.

What?

HEDDA.

[*Going to the glass door.*] Nothing.

TESMAN.

Oh, all right.

[*He goes through the inner room, out to the right.*

BRACK.

What bonnet were you talking about?

HEDDA.

Oh, it was a little episode with Miss Tesman this morning. She had laid down her bonnet on the chair there—[*Looks at him and smiles.*]—and I pretended to think it was the servant's.

BRACK.

[*Shaking his head.*] Now my dear Mrs. Hedda, how could you do such a thing? To that excellent old lady, too!

HEDDA.

[*Nervously crossing the room.*] Well, you see—these impulses come over me all of a sudden; and I cannot resist them. [*Throws herself down in the easy-chair by the stove.*] Oh, I don't know how to explain it.

BRACK.

[*Behind the easy-chair.*] You are not really happy—that is at the bottom of it.

HEDDA.

[*Looking straight before her.*] I know of no reason why I should be—happy. Perhaps you can give me one?

BRACK.

Well—amongst other things, because you have got exactly the home you had set your heart on.

HEDDA.

[*Looks up at him and laughs.*] Do you too believe in that legend?

BRACK.

Is there nothing in it, then?

HEDDA.

Oh yes, there is something in it.

BRACK.

Well?

HEDDA.

There is this in it, that I made use of Tesman to see me home from evening parties last summer——

BRACK.

I, unfortunately, had to go quite a different way.

HEDDA.

That's true. I know you were going a different way last summer.

BRACK.

[*Laughing.*] Oh fie, Mrs. Hedda! Well, then —you and Tesman——?

HEDDA.

Well, we happened to pass here one evening; Tesman, poor fellow, was writhing in the agony of having to find conversation; so I took pity on the learned man——

BRACK.

[*Smiles doubtfully.*] You took pity? H'm——

HEDDA.

Yes, I really did. And so—to help him out of his torment—I happened to say, in pure thoughtlessness, that I should like to live in this villa.

BRACK.

No more than that?

HEDDA.

Not that evening.

BRACK.

But afterwards?

HEDDA.

Yes, my thoughtlessness had consequences, my dear Judge.

BRACK.

Unfortunately that too often happens, Mrs. Hedda.

HEDDA.

Thanks! So you see it was this enthusiasm for Secretary Falk's villa that first constituted a bond of sympathy between George Tesman and me. From that came our engagement and our marriage, and our wedding journey, and all the rest of it. Well, well, my dear Judge—as you make your bed so you must lie, I could almost say.

BRACK.

This is exquisite! And you really cared not a rap about it all the time?

HEDDA.

No, heaven knows I didn't.

BRACK.

But now? Now that we have made it so homelike for you?

HEDDA.

Uh—the rooms all seem to smell of lavender and dried rose-leaves.—But perhaps it's Aunt Julia that has brought that scent with her.

BRACK.

[*Laughing.*] No, I think it must be a legacy from the late Mrs. Secretary Falk.

HEDDA.

Yes, there is an odour of mortality about it. It reminds me of a bouquet—the day after the ball. [*Clasps her hands behind her head, leans back in her chair and looks at him.*] Oh, my dear Judge—you cannot imagine how horribly I shall bore myself here.

BRACK.

Why should not you, too, find some sort of vocation in life, Mrs. Hedda?

HEDDA.

A vocation—that should attract me?

BRACK.

If possible, of course.

HEDDA.

Heaven knows what sort of a vocation that could be. I often wonder whether—— [*Breaking off.*] But that would never do either.

BRACK.

Who can tell? Let me hear what it is.

HEDDA.

Whether I might not get Tesman to go into politics, I mean.

BRACK.

[*Laughing.*] Tesman? No really now, political life is not the thing for him—not at all in his line.

HEDDA.

No, I daresay not.—But if I could get him into it all the same?

BRACK.

Why—what satisfaction could you find in that? If he is not fitted for that sort of thing, why should you want to drive him into it?

HEDDA.

Because I am bored, I tell you! [*After a pause.*] So you think it quite out of the question that Tesman should ever get into the ministry?

BRACK.

H'm—you see, my dear Mrs. Hedda—to get into the ministry, he would have to be a tolerably rich man.

HEDDA.

[*Rising impatiently.*] Yes, there we have it! It is this genteel poverty I have managed to drop into——! [*Crosses the room.*] That is what makes life so pitiable! So utterly ludicrous!—For that's what it is.

BRACK.

Now *I* should say the fault lay elsewhere.

HEDDA.

Where, then?

BRACK.

You have never gone through any really stimulating experience.

HEDDA.

Anything serious, you mean?

BRACK.

Yes, you may call it so. But now you may perhaps have one in store.

HEDDA.

[*Tossing her head.*] Oh, you're thinking of the annoyances about this wretched professorship! But that must be Tesman's own affair. I assure you I shall not waste a thought upon it.

BRACK.

No, no, I daresay not. But suppose now that what people call—in elegant language—a solemn responsibility were to come upon you? [*Smiling.*] A new responsibility, Mrs. Hedda?

HEDDA.

[*Angrily.*] Be quiet! Nothing of that sort will ever happen!

BRACK.

[*Warily.*] We will speak of this again a year hence—at the very outside.

HEDDA.

[*Curtly.*] I have no turn for anything of the sort, Judge Brack. No responsibilities for me!

BRACK.

Are you so unlike the generality of women as to have no turn for duties which——?

HEDDA.

[*Beside the glass door.*] Oh, be quiet, I tell you! —I often think there is only one thing in the world I have any turn for.

BRACK.

[*Drawing near to her.*] And what is that, if may ask?

HEDDA.

[*Stands looking out.*] Boring myself to death. Now you know it. [*Turns, looks towards the inner room, and laughs.*] Yes, as I thought! Here comes the Professor.

BRACK.

[*Softly, in a tone of warning.*] Come, come, come, Mrs. Hedda!

GEORGE TESMAN, *dressed for the party, with his gloves and hat in his hand, enters from the right through the inner room.*

TESMAN.

Hedda, has no message come from Eilert Lövborg? Eh?

HEDDA.

No.

TESMAN.

Then you'll see he'll be here presently.

BRACK.

Do you really think he will come?

TESMAN.

Yes, I am almost sure of it. For what you were telling us this morning must have been a mere floating rumour.

BRACK.

You think so?

TESMAN.

At any rate, Aunt Julia said she did not believe for a moment that he would ever stand in my way again. Fancy that!

BRACK.

Well then, that's all right.

TESMAN.

[*Placing his hat and gloves on a chair on the right.*] Yes, but you must really let me wait for him as long as possible.

BRACK.

We have plenty of time yet. None of my guests will arrive before seven or half-past.

TESMAN.

Then meanwhile we can keep Hedda company, and see what happens. Eh?

HEDDA.

[*Placing* BRACK's *hat and overcoat upon the corner settee.*] And at the worst Mr. Lövborg can remain here with me.

BRACK.

[*Offering to take his things.*] Oh, allow me, Mrs. Tesman!—What do you mean by "At the worst"?

HEDDA.

If he won't go with you and Tesman.

TESMAN.

[*Looks dubiously at her.*] But, Hedda dear—do you think it would quite do for him to remain with you? Eh? Remember, Aunt Julia can't come.

HEDDA.

No, but Mrs. Elvsted is coming. We three can have a cup of tea together.

TESMAN.

Oh yes, that will be all right.

BRACK.

[*Smiling.*] And that would perhaps be the safest plan for him.

HEDDA.

Why so?

BRACK.

Well, you know, Mrs. Tesman, how you used to gird at my little bachelor parties. You declared they were adapted only for men of the strictest principles.

HEDDA.

But no doubt Mr. Lövborg's principles are strict enough now. A converted sinner——

[BERTA *appears at the hall door.*

BERTA.

There's a gentleman asking if you are at home, ma'am——

HEDDA.

Well, show him in.

TESMAN.

[*Softly.*] I'm sure it is he! Fancy that!

EILERT LÖVBORG *enters from the hall. He is slim and lean; of the same age as* TESMAN, *but looks older and somewhat worn-out. His hair and beard are of a blackish brown, his face long and pale, but with patches of colour on the cheek-bones. He is dressed in a well-cut black visiting suit, quite new. He has dark gloves and a silk hat. He stops near the door, and makes a rapid bow, seeming somewhat embarrassed.*

TESMAN.

[*Goes up to him and shakes him warmly by the hand.*] Well, my dear Eilert—so at last we meet again!

EILERT LÖVBORG.

[*Speaks in a subdued voice.*] Thanks for your letter, Tesman. [*Approaching* HEDDA.] Will you too shake hands with me, Mrs. Tesman?

HEDDA.

[*Taking his hand.*] I am glad to see you, Mr. Lövborg. [*With a motion of her hand.*] I don't know whether you two gentlemen——?

LÖVBORG.

[*Bowing slightly.*] Judge Brack, I think.

BRACK.

[*Doing likewise.*] Oh yes,—in the old days——

TESMAN.

[*To* LÖVBORG, *with his hands on his shoulders.*] And now you must make yourself entirely at home, Eilert! Musn't he, Hedda?—For I hear you are going to settle in town again? Eh?

LÖVBORG.

Yes, I am.

TESMAN.

Quite right, quite right. Let me tell you, I have got hold of your new book; but I haven't had time to read it yet.

LÖVBORG.

You may spare yourself the trouble.

TESMAN.

Why so?

LÖVBORG.

Because there is very little in it.

TESMAN.

Just fancy—how can you say so?

BRACK.

But it has been very much praised, I hear.

LÖVBORG.

That was what I wanted; so I put nothing into the book but what every one would agree with.

BRACK.

Very wise of you.

TESMAN.

Well but, my dear Eilert——!

LÖVBORG.

For now I mean to win myself a position again—to make a fresh start.

TESMAN.

[*A little embarrassed.*] Ah, that is what you wish to do? Eh?

LÖVBORG.

[*Smiling, lays down his hat, and draws a packet, wrapped in paper, from his coat pocket.*] But when this one appears, George Tesman, you will have to read it. For this is the real book—the book I have put my true self into.

TESMAN.

Indeed? And what is it?

LÖVBORG.

It is the continuation.

TESMAN.

The continuation? Of what?

LÖVBORG.

Of the book.

TESMAN.

Of the new book?

LÖVBORG.

Of course

TESMAN.

Why, my dear Eilert—does it not come down to our own days?

LÖVBORG.

Yes, it does; and this one deals with the future.

TESMAN.

With the future! But, good heavens, we know nothing of the future!

LÖVBORG.

No; but there is a thing or two to be said about it all the same. [*Opens the packet.*] Look here——

TESMAN.

Why, that's not your handwriting.

LÖVBORG.

I dictated it. [*Turning over the pages.*] It falls into two sections. The first deals with the civilising forces of the future. And here is the second —[*running through the pages towards the end*]—forecasting the probable line of development.

TESMAN.

How odd now! I should never have thought of writing anything of that sort.

HEDDA

[*At the glass door, drumming on the pane.*] H'm——. I daresay not.

LÖVBORG.

[*Replacing the manuscript in its paper and laying the packet on the table.*] I brought it, thinking I might read you a little of it this evening.

TESMAN.

That was very good of you, Eilert. But this evening——? [*Looking at* BRACK.] I don't quite see how we can manage it——

LÖVBORG.

Well then, some other time. There is no hurry.

BRACK.

I must tell you, Mr. Lövborg—there is a little gathering at my house this evening—mainly in honour of Tesman, you know——

LÖVBORG.

[*Looking for his hat.*] Oh—then I won't detain you——

BRACK.

No, but listen—will you not do me the favour of joining us?

LÖVBORG.

[*Curtly and decidedly.*] No, I can't—thank you very much.

BRACK.

Oh, nonsense—do! We shall be quite a select little circle. And I assure you we shall have a "lively time," as Mrs. Hed—as Mrs. Tesman says.

LÖVBORG.

I have no doubt of it. But nevertheless——

BRACK.

And then you might bring your manuscript with you, and read it to Tesman at my house. I could give you a room to yourselves.

TESMAN.

Yes, think of that, Eilert,—why shouldn't you? Eh?

HEDDA.

[*Interposing.*] But, Tesman, if Mr. Lövborg would really rather not! I am sure Mr. Lövborg is much more inclined to remain here and have supper with me.

LÖVBORG.

[*Looking at her.*] With you, Mrs. Tesman?

HEDDA.

And with Mrs. Elvsted.

LÖVBORG.

Ah—— [*Lightly.*] I saw her for a moment this morning.

HEDDA.

Did you? Well, she is coming this evening. So you see you are almost bound to remain, Mr. Lövborg, or she will have no one to see her home.

LÖVBORG.

That's true. Many thanks, Mrs. Tesman—in that case I will remain.

HEDDA.

Then I have one or two orders to give the servant——

[*She goes to the hall door and rings.* BERTA *enters.* HEDDA *talks to her in a whisper, and points towards the inner room.* BERTA *nods and goes out again.*

TESMAN.

[*At the same time, to* LÖVBORG.] Tell me, Eilert—is it this new subject—the future—that you are going to lecture about?

LÖVBORG.

Yes.

TESMAN.

They told me at the bookseller's that you are going to deliver a course of lectures this autumn.

LÖVBORG.

That is my intention. I hope you won't take it ill, Tesman.

TESMAN.

Oh no, not in the least! But——?

LÖVBORG.

I can quite understand that it must be disagreeable to you.

TESMAN.

[*Cast down.*] Oh, I can't expect you, out of consideration for me, to——

LÖVBORG.

But I shall wait till you have received your appointment.

TESMAN.

Will you wait? Yes but—yes but—are you not going to compete with me? Eh?

LÖVBORG.

No; it is only the moral victory I care for.

TESMAN.

Why, bless me—then Aunt Julia was right after all! Oh yes—I knew it! Hedda! Just fancy—Eilert Lövborg is not going to stand in our way!

HEDDA.

[*Curtly.*] Our way? Pray leave me out of the question.

[*She goes up towards the inner room, where* BERTA *is placing a tray with decanters and glasses on the table.* HEDDA *nods approval, and comes forward again.* BERTA *goes out.*

TESMAN.

[*At the same time.*] And you, Judge Brack—what do you say to this? Eh?

BRACK.

Well, I say that a moral victory—h'm—may be all very fine——

TESMAN.

Yes, certainly. But all the same——

HEDDA.

[*Looking at* TESMAN *with a cold smile.*] You

stand there looking as if you were thunder-struck——

TESMAN.

Yes—so I am—I almost think——

BRACK.

Don't you see, Mrs. Tesman, a thunderstorm has just passed over?

HEDDA.

[*Pointing towards the inner room.*] Will you not take a glass of cold punch, gentlemen?

BRACK.

[*Looking at his watch.*] A stirrup-cup? Yes, it wouldn't come amiss.

TESMAN.

A capital idea, Hedda! Just the thing! Now that the weight has been taken off my mind——

HEDDA.

Will you not join them, Mr. Lövborg?

LÖVBORG.

[*With a gesture of refusal.*] No, thank you. Nothing for me.

BRACK.

Why bless me—cold punch is surely not poison.

LÖVBORG.

Perhaps not for every one.

HEDDA.

I will keep Mr. Lövborg company in the meantime.

TESMAN.

Yes, yes, Hedda dear, do.

[*He and* BRACK *go into the inner room, seat themselves, drink punch, smoke cigarettes, and carry on a lively conversation during what follows.* EILERT LÖVBORG *remains standing beside the stove.* HEDDA *goes to the writing-table.*

HEDDA.

[*Raising her voice a little.*] Do you care to look at some photographs, Mr. Lövborg? You know Tesman and I made a tour in the Tyrol on our way home?

[*She takes up an album, and places it on the table beside the sofa, in the further corner of which she seats herself.* EILERT LÖVBORG *approaches, stops, aud looks at her. Then he takes a chair and seats himself to her left, with his back towards the inner room.*

HEDDA.

[*Opening the album.*] Do you see this range of mountains, Mr. Lövborg? It's the Ortler group. Tesman has written the name underneath. Here it is: "The Ortler group near Meran."

LÖVBORG.

[*Who has never taken his eyes off her, says softly and slowly:*] Hedda—Gabler!

HEDDA.

[*Glancing hastily at him.*] Ah! Hush!

LÖVBORG.

[*Repeats softly.*] Hedda Gabler!

HEDDA.

[*Looking at the album.*] That was my name in the old days—when we two knew each other.

LÖVBORG.

And I must teach myself never to say Hedda Gabler again—never, as long as I live.

HEDDA.

[*Still turning over the pages.*] Yes, you must. And I think you ought to practise in time. The sooner the better, I should say.

LÖVBORG.

[*In a tone of indignation.*] Hedda Gabler married? And married to—George Tesman!

HEDDA.

Yes—so the world goes.

LÖVBORG.

Oh, Hedda, Hedda—how could you[1] throw yourself away!

HEDDA.

[*Looks sharply at him.*] What? I can't allow this!

LÖVBORG.

What do you mean?

[TESMAN *comes into the room and goes towards the sofa.*

HEDDA.

[*Hears him coming and says in an indifferent tone.*] And this is a view from the Val d'Ampezzo, Mr.

[1] He uses the familiar *du*.

Lövborg. Just look at these peaks! [*Looks affectionately up at* TESMAN.] What's the name of these curious peaks, dear?

TESMAN.

Let me see. Oh, those are the Dolomites.

HEDDA.

Yes, that's it!—Those are the Dolomites, Mr. Lövborg.

TESMAN.

Hedda dear,—I only wanted to ask whether I shouldn't bring you a little punch after all? For yourself at any rate—eh?

HEDDA.

Yes, do, please; and perhaps a few biscuits.

TESMAN.

No cigarettes?

HEDDA.

No.

TESMAN.

Very well.

[*He goes into the inner room and out to the right.* BRACK *sits in the inner room, and keeps an eye from time to time on* HEDDA *and* LÖVBORG.

LÖVBORG.

[*Softly, as before.*] Answer me, Hedda—how could you go and do this?

HEDDA.

[*Apparently absorbed in the album.*] If you continue to say *du* to me I won't talk to you.

LÖVBORG.

May I not say *du* even when we are alone?

HEDDA.

No. You may think it; but you mustn't say it.

LÖVBORG.

Ah, I understand. It is an offence against George Tesman, whom you[1]—love.

HEDDA.

[*Glances at him and smiles.*] Love? What an idea!

LÖVBORG.

You don't love him then!

HEDDA.

But I won't hear of any sort of unfaithfulness! Remember that.

LÖVBORG.

Hedda—answer me one thing——

HEDDA.

Hush!

[TESMAN *enters with a small tray from the inner room.*

TESMAN.

Here you are! Isn't this tempting?

[*He puts the tray on the table.*

HEDDA.

Why do you bring it yourself?

[1] From this point onward Lövborg uses the formal *De.*

TESMAN.

[*Filling the glasses.*] Because I think it's such fun to wait upon you, Hedda.

HEDDA.

But you have poured out two glasses. Mr. Lövborg said he wouldn't have any——

TESMAN.

No, but Mrs. Elvsted will soon be here, won't she?

HEDDA.

Yes, by-the-bye—Mrs. Elvsted——

TESMAN.

Had you forgotten her? Eh?

HEDDA.

We were so absorbed in these photographs. [*Shows him a picture.*] Do you remember this little village?

TESMAN.

Oh, it's that one just below the Brenner Pass. It was there we passed the night——

HEDDA.

——and met that lively party of tourists.

TESMAN.

Yes, that was the place. Fancy—if we could only have had you with us, Eilert! Eh?

[*He returns to the inner room and sits beside* BRACK.

LÖVBORG.

Answer me this one thing, Hedda——

HEDDA.

Well?

LÖVBORG.

Was there no love in your friendship for me either? Not a spark—not a tinge of love in it?

HEDDA.

I wonder if there was? To me it seems as though we were two good comrades—two thoroughly intimate friends. [*Smilingly.*] You especially were frankness itself.

LÖVBORG.

It was you that made me so.

HEDDA.

As I look back upon it all, I think there was really something beautiful, something fascinating —something daring—in—in that secret intimacy —that comradeship which no living creature so much as dreamed of.

LÖVBORG.

Yes, yes, Hedda! Was there not?—When I used to come to your father's in the afternoon—and the General sat over at the window reading his papers—with his back towards us——

HEDDA.

And we two on the corner sofa——

LÖVBORG.

Always with the same illustrated paper before us——

HEDDA.

For want of an album, yes.

LÖVBORG.

Yes, Hedda, and when I made my confessions to you—told you about myself, things that at that time no one else knew! There I would sit and tell you of my escapades—my days and nights of devilment. Oh, Hedda—what was the power in you that forced me to confess these things?

HEDDA.

Do you think it was any power in me?

LÖVBORG.

How else can I explain it? And all those—those roundabout questions you used to put to me——

HEDDA.

Which you understood so particularly well——

LÖVBORG.

How could you sit and question me like that? Question me quite frankly——

HEDDA.

In roundabout terms, please observe.

LÖVBORG.

Yes, but frankly nevertheless. Cross-question me about—all that sort of thing?

HEDDA.

And how could you answer, Mr. Lövborg?

LÖVBORG.

Yes, that is just what I can't understand—in looking back upon it. But tell me now, Hedda—was there not love at the bottom of our friendship? On your side, did you not feel as though you might purge my stains away—if I made you my confessor? Was it not so?

HEDDA.

No, not quite.

LÖVBORG.

What was your motive, then?

HEDDA.

Do you think it quite incomprehensible that a young girl—when it can be done—without any one knowing——

LÖVBORG.

Well?

HEDDA.

——should be glad to have a peep, now and then, into a world which——

LÖVBORG.

Which——?

HEDDA.

——which she is forbidden to know anything about?

LÖVBORG.

So that was it?

HEDDA.

Partly. Partly—I almost think.

LÖVBORG.

Comradeship in the thirst for life. But why should not that, at any rate, have continued?

HEDDA.

The fault was yours.

LÖVBORG.

It was you that broke with me.

HEDDA.

Yes, when our friendship threatened to develop into something more serious. Shame upon you, Eilert Lövborg! How could you think of wronging your—your frank comrade?

LÖVBORG.

[*Clenching his hands.*] Oh, why did you not carry out your threat? Why did you not shoot me down?

HEDDA.

Because I have such a dread of scandal.

LÖVBORG.

Yes, Hedda, you are a coward at heart.

HEDDA.

A terrible coward. [*Changing her tone.*] But it was a lucky thing for you. And now you have found ample consolation at the Elvsteds'.

LÖVBORG.

I know what Thea has confided to you.

HEDDA.

And perhaps you have confided to her something about us?

LÖVBORG.

Not a word. She is too stupid to understand anything of that sort.

HEDDA.

Stupid?

LÖVBORG.

She is stupid about matters of that sort.

HEDDA.

And I am cowardly. [*Bends over towards him, without looking him in the face, and says more softly :*] But now I will confide something to you.

LÖVBORG.

[*Eagerly.*] Well?

HEDDA.

The fact that I dared not shoot you down——

LÖVBORG.

Yes!

HEDDA.

——that was not my most arrant cowardice—that evening.

LÖVBORG.

[*Looks at her a moment, understands, and whispers passionately.*] Oh, Hedda! Hedda Gabler! Now I begin to see a hidden reason beneath our comradeship! You[1] and I——! After all, then, it was your craving for life——

HEDDA.

[*Softly, with a sharp glance.*] Take care! Believe nothing of the sort!

[*Twilight has begun to fall. The hall door is opened from without by* BERTA.

HEDDA.

[*Closes the album with a bang and calls smilingly :*] Ah, at last! My darling Thea,—come along!

[1] In this speech he once more says *du*. Hedda addresses him throughout as *De*.

MRS. ELVSTED *enters from the hall. She is in evening dress. The door is closed behind her.*

HEDDA.

[*On the sofa, stretches out her arms towards her.*] My sweet Thea—you can't think how I have been longing for you!

[MRS. ELVSTED, *in passing, exchanges slight salutations with the gentlemen in the inner room, then goes up to the table and gives* HEDDA *her hand.* EILERT LÖVBORG *has risen. He and* MRS. ELVSTED *greet each other with a silent nod.*

MRS. ELVSTED.

Ought I to go in and talk to your husband for a moment?

HEDDA.

Oh, not at all. Leave those two alone. They will soon be going.

MRS. ELVSTED.

Are they going out?

HEDDA.

Yes, to a supper-party.

MRS. ELVSTED.

[*Quickly, to* LÖVBORG.] Not you?

LÖVBORG.

No.

HEDDA.

Mr. Lövborg remains with us.

MRS. ELVSTED.

[*Takes a chair and is about to seat herself at his side.*] Oh, how nice it is here!

HEDDA.

No, thank you, my little Thea! Not there! You'll be good enough to come over here to me. I will sit between you.

MRS. ELVSTED.

Yes, just as you please.

[*She goes round the table and seats herself on the sofa on* HEDDA'S *right.* LÖVBORG *re-seats himself on his chair.*

LÖVBORG.

[*After a short pause, to* HEDDA.] Is not she lovely to look at?

HEDDA.

[*Lightly stroking her hair.*] Only to look at?

LÖVBORG.

Yes. For we two—she and I—we are two real comrades. We have absolute faith in each other; so we can sit and talk with perfect frankness——

HEDDA.

Not round about, Mr. Lövborg?

LÖVBORG.

Well——

MRS. ELVSTED.

[*Softly clinging close to* HEDDA.] Oh, how happy I am, Hedda! For, only think, he says I have inspired him too

HEDDA.

[*Looks at her with a smile.*] Ah! Does he say that, dear?

LÖVBORG.

And then she is so brave, Mrs. Tesman!

MRS. ELVSTED.

Good heavens—am I brave?

LÖVBORG.

Exceedingly—where your comrade is concerned.

HEDDA.

Ah yes—courage! If one only had that!

LÖVBORG.

What then? What do you mean?

HEDDA.

Then life would perhaps be liveable, after all. [*With a sudden change of tone.*] But now, my dearest Thea, you really must have a glass of cold punch.

MRS. ELVSTED.

No, thanks—I never take anything of that kind.

HEDDA.

Well then, you, Mr. Lövborg.

LÖVBORG.

Nor I, thank you.

MRS. ELVSTED.

No, he doesn't either.

HEDDA.

[*Looks fixedly at him.*] But if I say you shall?

LÖVBORG.

It would be no use.

HEDDA.

[*Laughing.*] Then I, poor creature, have no sort of power over you?

LÖVBORG.

Not in that respect.

HEDDA.

But seriously, I think you ought to—for your own sake.

MRS. ELVSTED.

Why, Hedda——!

LÖVBORG.

How so?

HEDDA.

Or rather on account of other people.

LÖVBORG.

Indeed?

HEDDA.

Otherwise people might be apt to suspect that —in your heart of hearts—you did not feel quite secure—quite confident in yourself.

MRS. ELVSTED.

[*Softly.*] Oh please, Hedda——:

LÖVBORG.

People may suspect what they like—for the present.

MRS. ELVSTED.

[*Joyfully.*] Yes, let them !

HEDDA.

I saw it plainly in Judge Brack's face a moment ago.

LÖVBORG.

What did you see ?

HEDDA.

His contemptuous smile, when you dared not go with them into the inner room.

LÖVBORG.

Dared not ? Of course I preferred to stop here and talk to you.

MRS. ELVSTED.

What could be more natural, Hedda ?

HEDDA.

But the Judge could not guess that. And I saw, too, the way he smiled and glanced at Tesman when you dared not accept his invitation to this wretched little supper-party of his.

LÖVBORG.

Dared not ! Do you say I dared not ?

HEDDA.

I don't say so. But that was how Judge Brack understood it.

LÖVBORG.

Well, let him.

HEDDA.

Then you are not going with them ?

LÖVBORG.

I will stay here with you and Thea.

MRS. ELVSTED.

Yes, Hedda—how can you doubt that?

HEDDA.

[*Smiles and nods approvingly to* LÖVBORG.] Firm as a rock! Faithful to your principles, now and for ever! Ah, that is how a man should be! [*Turns to* MRS. ELVSTED *and caresses her.*] Well now, what did I tell you, when you came to us this morning in such a state of distraction——

LÖVBORG.

[*Surprised.*] Distraction!

MRS. ELVSTED.

[*Terrified.*] Hedda—oh Hedda——!

HEDDA.

You can see for yourself! You haven't the slightest reason to be in such mortal terror——[*Interrupting herself.*] There! Now we can all three enjoy ourselves!

LÖVBORG.

[*Who has given a start.*] Ah—what is all this, Mrs. Tesman?

MRS. ELVSTED.

Oh my God, Hedda! What are you saying? What are you doing?

HEDDA.

Don't get excited! That horrid Judge Brack is sitting watching you.

LÖVBORG.

So she was in mortal terror! On my account!

MRS. ELVSTED.

[*Softly and piteously.*] Oh, Hedda—now you have ruined everything!

LÖVBORG.

[*Looks fixedly at her for a moment. His face is distorted.*] So that was my comrade's frank confidence in me?

MRS. ELVSTED.

[*Imploringly.*] Oh, my dearest friend—only let me tell you——

LÖVBORG.

[*Takes one of the glasses of punch, raises it to his lips, and says in a low, husky voice.*] Your health, Thea!

[*He empties the glass, puts it down, and takes the second.*

MRS. ELVSTED.

[*Softly.*] Oh, Hedda, Hedda—how could you do this?

HEDDA.

I do it? *I*? Are you crazy?

LÖVBORG.

Here's to your health too, Mrs. Tesman. Thanks for the truth Hurrah for the truth!

[*He empties the glass and is about to re-fill it.*

HEDDA.

[*Lays her hand on his arm.*] Come, come—no more for the present. Remember you are going out to supper.

MRS. ELVSTED.

No, no, no!

HEDDA.

Hush! They are sitting watching you.

LÖVBORG.

[*Putting down the glass.*] Now, Thea—tell me the truth——

MRS. ELVSTED.

Yes.

LÖVBORG.

Did your husband know that you had come after me?

MRS. ELVSTED.

[*Wringing her hands.*] Oh, Hedda—do you hear what he is asking?

LÖVBORG.

Was it arranged between you and him that you were to come to town and look after me? Perhaps it was the Sheriff himself that urged you to come? Aha, my dear—no doubt he wanted my help in his office! Or was it at the card-table that he missed me?

MRS. ELVSTED.

[*Softly, in agony.*] Oh, Lövborg, Lövborg——!

LÖVBORG.

[*Seizes a glass and is on the point of filling it.*] Here's a glass for the old Sheriff too!

HEDDA.

[*Preventing him.*] No more just now. Remember, you have to read your manuscript to Tesman.

LÖVBORG.

[*Calmly, putting down the glass.*] It was stupid of me all this, Thea—to take it in this way, I mean. Don't be angry with me, my dear, dear comrade. You shall see—both you and the others—that if I was fallen once—now I have risen again! Thanks to you, Thea.

MRS. ELVSTED.

[*Radiant with joy.*] Oh, heaven be praised——!

[BRACK *has in the meantime looked at his watch. He and* TESMAN *rise and come into the drawing-room.*

BRACK.

[*Takes his hat and overcoat.*] Well, Mrs. Tesman, our time has come.

HEDDA.

I suppose it has.

LÖVBORG.

[*Rising.*] Mine too, Judge Brack.

MRS. ELVSTED.

[*Softly and imploringly.*] Oh, Lövborg, don't do it!

HEDDA.

[*Pinching her arm.*] They can hear you!

MRS. ELVSTED.

[*With a suppressed shriek.*] Ow!

LÖVBORG.

[*To* BRACK.] You were good enough to invite me.

BRACK.

Well, are you coming after all?

LÖVBORG.

Yes, many thanks.

BRACK.

I'm delighted——

LÖVBORG.

[*To* TESMAN, *putting the parcel of MS. in his pocket.*] I should like to show you one or two things before I send it to the printers.

TESMAN.

Fancy—that will be delightful. But, Hedda dear, how is Mrs. Elvsted to get home? Eh?

HEDDA.

Oh, that can be managed somehow.

LÖVBORG.

[*Looking towards the ladies.*] Mrs. Elvsted? Of course, I'll come again and fetch her. [*Approaching.*] At ten or thereabouts, Mrs. Tesman? Will that do?

HEDDA.

Certainly. That will do capitally.

TESMAN.

Well, then, that's all right. But you must not expect me so early, Hedda.

HEDDA.

Oh, you may stop as long—as long as ever you please.

MRS. ELVSTED.

[*Trying to conceal her anxiety.*] Well then, Mr. Lövborg—I shall remain here until you come.

LÖVBORG.

[*With his hat in his hand.*] Pray do, Mrs. Elvsted.

BRACK.

And now off goes the excursion train, gentlemen! I hope we shall have a lively time, as a certain fair lady puts it.

HEDDA.

Ah, if only the fair lady could be present unseen——!

BRACK.

Why unseen?

HEDDA.

In order to hear a little of your liveliness at first hand, Judge Brack.

BRACK.

[*Laughing.*] I should not advise the fair lady to try it.

TESMAN.

[*Also laughing.*] Come, you're a nice one Hedda! Fancy that!

BRACK.

Well, good-bye, good-bye, ladies.

LÖVBORG.

[*Bowing.*] About ten o'clock, then.

[BRACK, LÖVBORG, *and* TESMAN *go out by the hall door. At the same time,* BERTA *enters from the inner room with a lighted lamp, which she places on the drawing-room table; she goes out by the way she came.*

MRS. ELVSTED.

[*Who has risen and is wandering restlessly about the room.*] Hedda—Hedda—what will come of all this?

HEDDA.

At ten o'clock—he will be here. I can see him already—with vine-leaves in his hair—flushed and fearless——

MRS. ELVSTED.

Oh, I hope he may.

HEDDA.

And then, you see—then he will have regained control over himself. Then he will be a free man for all his days.

MRS. ELVSTED.

Oh God!—if he would only come as you see him now!

HEDDA.

He will come as I see him—so, and not otherwise! [*Rises and approaches* THEA.] You may doubt him as long as you please; *I* believe in him. And now we will try——

MRS. ELVSTED.

You have some hidden motive in this, Hedda!

HEDDA.

Yes, I have. I want for once in my life to have power to mould a human destiny.

MRS. ELVSTED.

Have you not the power?

HEDDA.

I have not—and have never had it.

MRS. ELVSTED.

Not your husband's?

HEDDA.

Do you think that is worth the trouble? Oh, if you could only understand how poor I am. And fate has made you so rich! [*Clasps her passionately in her arms.*] I think I must burn your hair off, after all.

MRS. ELVSTED.

Let me go! Let me go! I am afraid of you, Hedda!

BERTA.

[*In the middle doorway.*] Tea is laid in the dining-room, ma'am.

HEDDA.

Very well. We are coming.

MRS. ELVSTED.

No, no, no! I would rather go home alone! At once!

HEDDA.

Nonsense! First you shall have a cup of tea, you little stupid. And then—at ten o'clock—Eilert Lövborg will be here—with vine-leaves in his hair.

[*She drags* MRS. ELVSTED *almost by force towards the middle doorway.*

ACT THIRD.

The room at the TESMANS'. *The curtains are drawn over the middle doorway, and also over the glass door. The lamp, half turned down, and with a shade over it, is burning on the table. In the stove, the door of which stands open, there has been a fire, which is now nearly burnt out.*

MRS. ELVSTED, *wrapped in a large shawl, and with her feet upon a foot-rest, sits close to the stove, sunk back in the arm-chair.* HEDDA, *fully dressed, lies sleeping upon the sofa, with a sofa-blanket over her.*

MRS. ELVSTED.

[*After a pause, suddenly sits up in her chair, and listens eagerly. Then she sinks back again wearily, moaning to herself.*] Not yet!—Oh God—oh God —not yet!

BERTA *slips cautiously in by the hall door. She has a letter in her hand.*

MRS. ELVSTED.

[*Turns and whispers eagerly.*] Well—has any one come?

BERTA.

[*Softly.* Yes, a girl has just brought this letter.

MRS. ELVSTED.

[*Quickly, holding out her hand.*] A letter! Give it to me!

BERTA.

No, it's for Dr. Tesman, ma'am.

MRS. ELVSTED.

Oh, indeed.

BERTA.

It was Miss Tesman's servant that brought it. I'll lay it here on the table.

MRS. ELVSTED.

Yes, do.

BERTA.

[*Laying down the letter.*] I think I had better put out the lamp. It's smoking.

MRS. ELVSTED.

Yes, put it out. It must soon be daylight now.

BERTA.

[*Putting out the lamp.*] It is daylight already, ma'am.

MRS. ELVSTED.

Yes, broad day! And no one come back yet——!

BERTA.

Lord bless you, ma'am—I guessed how it would be.

MRS. ELVSTED.

You guessed?

BERTA.

Yes, when I saw that a certain person had come

back to town—and that he went off with them. For we've heard enough about that gentleman before now.

MRS. ELVSTED.

Don't speak so loud. You will waken Mrs. Tesman.

BERTA.

[*Looks towards the sofa and sighs.*] No, no—let her sleep, poor thing. Shan't I put some wood on the fire?

MRS. ELVSTED.

Thanks, not for me.

BERTA.

Oh, very well.

[*She goes softly out by the hall door.*

HEDDA.

[*Is wakened by the shutting of the door, and looks up.*] What's that——?

MRS. ELVSTED.

It was only the servant——

HEDDA.

[*Looking about her.*] Oh, we're here——! Yes, now I remember. [*Sits erect upon the sofa, stretches herself, and rubs her eyes.*] What o'clock is it, Thea?

MRS. ELVSTED.

[*Looks at her watch.*] It's past seven.

HEDDA.

When did Tesman come home?

MRS. ELVSTED.

He has not come.

HEDDA.

Not come home yet?

MRS. ELVSTED.

[*Rising.*] No one has come.

HEDDA.

Think of our watching and waiting here till four in the morning——

MRS. ELVSTED.

[*Wringing her hands.*] And how I watched and waited for him!

HEDDA.

[*Yawns, and says with her hand before her mouth.*] Well well—we might have spared ourselves the trouble.

MRS. ELVSTED.

Did you get a little sleep?

HEDDA.

Oh yes; I believe I have slept pretty well. Have you not?

MRS. ELVSTED.

Not for a moment. I couldn't, Hedda!—not to save my life.

HEDDA.

[*Rises and goes towards her.*] There there there! There's nothing to be so alarmed about. I understand quite well what has happened.

MRS. ELVSTED.

Well, what do you think? Won't you tell me?

HEDDA.

Why, of course it has been a very late affair at Judge Brack's——

MRS. ELVSTED.

Yes, yes—that is clear enough. But all the same——

HEDDA.

And then, you see, Tesman hasn't cared to come home and ring us up in the middle of the night. [*Laughing.*] Perhaps he wasn't inclined to show himself either—immediately after a jollification.

MRS. ELVSTED.

But in that case—where can he have gone?

HEDDA.

Of course he has gone to his Aunts' and slept there. They have his old room ready for him.

MRS. ELVSTED.

No, he can't be with them; for a letter has just come for him from Miss Tesman. There it lies.

HEDDA.

Indeed? [*Looks at the address.*] Why yes, it's addressed in Aunt Julia's own hand. Well then, he has remained at Judge Brack's. And as for Eilert Lövborg—he is sitting, with vine leaves in his hair, reading his manuscript.

MRS. ELVSTED.

Oh Hedda, you are just saying things you don't believe a bit.

HEDDA.

You really are a little blockhead, Thea.

MRS. ELVSTED.

Oh yes, I suppose I am.

HEDDA.

And how mortally tired you look.

MRS. ELVSTED.

Yes, I am mortally tired.

HEDDA.

Well then, you must do as I tell you. You must go into my room and lie down for a little while.

MRS. ELVSTED.

Oh no, no—I shouldn't be able to sleep.

HEDDA.

I am sure you would.

MRS. ELVSTED.

Well, but your husband is certain to come soon now; and then I want to know at once——

HEDDA.

I shall take care to let you know when he comes.

MRS. ELVSTED.

Do you promise me, Hedda?

HEDDA.

Yes, rely upon me. Just you go in and have a sleep in the meantime.

MRS. ELVSTED.

Thanks; then I'll try to.

[*She goes off through the inner room.*

[HEDDA *goes up to the glass door and draws back the curtains. The broad daylight streams into the room. Then she takes a little hand-glass from the writing-table, looks at herself in it, and arranges her hair. Next she goes to the hall door and presses the bell-button.*

BERTA *presently appears at the hall door.*

BERTA.

Did you want anything, ma'am?

HEDDA.

Yes; you must put some more wood in the stove. I am shivering.

BERTA.

Bless me—I'll make up the fire at once. [*She rakes the embers together and lays a piece of wood upon them; then stops and listens.*] That was a ring at the front door, ma'am.

HEDDA.

Then go to the door. I will look after the fire.

BERTA.

It'll soon burn up.

[*She goes out by the hall door.*

[HEDDA *kneels on the foot-rest and lays some more pieces of wood in the stove.*

After a short pause, GEORGE TESMAN *enters from the hall. He looks tired and rather serious. He steals on tiptoe towards the middle doorway and is about to slip through the curtains.*

HEDDA.

[*At the stove, without looking up.*] Good morning.

TESMAN.

[*Turns.*] Hedda! [*Approaching her.*] Good heavens—are you up so early? Eh?

HEDDA.

Yes, I am up very early this morning.

TESMAN.

And I never doubted you were still sound asleep! Fancy that, Hedda!

HEDDA.

Don't speak so loud. Mrs. Elvsted is resting in my room.

TESMAN.

Has Mrs. Elvsted been here all night?

HEDDA.

Yes, since no one came to fetch her.

TESMAN.

Ah, to be sure.

HEDDA.

[*Closes the door of the stove and rises.*] Well, did you enjoy yourselves at Judge Brack's?

TESMAN.

Have you been anxious about me? Eh?

HEDDA.

No, I should never think of being anxious. But I asked if you had enjoyed yourself.

TESMAN.

Oh yes,—for once in a way. Especially the beginning of the evening; for then Eilert read me part of his book. We arrived more than an hour too early—fancy that! And Brack had all sorts of arrangements to make—so Eilert read to me.

HEDDA.

[*Seating herself by the table on the right.*] Well? Tell me, then——

TESMAN.

[*Sitting on a footstool near the stove.*] Oh Hedda, you can't conceive what a book that is going to be! I believe it is one of the most remarkable things that have ever been written. Fancy that!

HEDDA.

Yes yes; I don't care about that——

TESMAN.

I must make a confession to you, Hedda. When he had finished reading—a horrid feeling came over me.

HEDDA.

A horrid feeling?

TESMAN.

I felt jealous of Eilert for having had it in him to write such a book. Only think, Hedda!

HEDDA.

Yes, yes, I am thinking!

TESMAN.

And then how pitiful to think that he—with all his gifts—should be irreclaimable, after all.

HEDDA.

I suppose you mean that he has more courage than the rest?

TESMAN.

No, not at all—I mean that he is incapable of taking his pleasures in moderation.

HEDDA.

And what came of it all—in the end?

TESMAN.

Well, to tell the truth, I think it might best be described as an orgie, Hedda.

HEDDA.

Had he vine-leaves in his hair?

TESMAN.

Vine-leaves? No, I saw nothing of the sort. But he made a long, rambling speech in honour of the woman who had inspired him in his work—that was the phrase he used.

HEDDA.

Did he name her?

TESMAN.

No, he didn't; but I can't help thinking he meant Mrs. Elvsted. You may be sure he did.

HEDDA.

Well—where did you part from him?

TESMAN.

On the way to town. We broke up—the last of us at any rate—all together; and Brack came with us to get a breath of fresh air. And then, you see, we agreed to take Eilert home; for he had had far more than was good for him.

HEDDA.

I daresay.

TESMAN.

But now comes the strange part of it, Hedda; or, I should rather say, the melancholy part of it. I declare I am almost ashamed—on Eilert's account—to tell you——

HEDDA.

Oh, go on——!

TESMAN.

Well, as we were getting near town, you see, I happened to drop a little behind the others. Only for a minute or two—fancy that!

HEDDA.

Yes yes yes, but——?

TESMAN.

And then, as I hurried after them—what do you think I found by the wayside? Eh?

HEDDA.

Oh, how should I know!

TESMAN.

You mustn't speak of it to a soul, Hedda! Do you hear! Promise me, for Eilert's sake. [*Draws a parcel, wrapped in paper, from his coat pocket.*] Fancy, dear—I found this.

HEDDA.

Is not that the parcel he had with him yesterday?

TESMAN.

Yes, it is the whole of his precious, irreplaceable manuscript! And he had gone and lost it, and knew nothing about it. Only fancy, Hedda! So deplorably——

HEDDA.

But why did you not give him back the parcel at once?

TESMAN.

I didn't dare to—in the state he was then in——

HEDDA.

Did you not tell any of the others that you had found it?

TESMAN.

Oh, far from it! You can surely understand that, for Eilert's sake, I wouldn't do that.

HEDDA.

So no one knows that Eilert Lövborg's manuscript is in your possession?

TESMAN.

No. And no one must know it

HEDDA.

Then what did you say to him afterwards?

TESMAN.

I didn't talk to him again at all; for when we got in among the streets, he and two or three of the others gave us the slip and disappeared. Fancy that!

HEDDA.

Indeed! They must have taken him home then.

TESMAN.

Yes, so it would appear. And Brack, too, left us.

HEDDA.

And what have you been doing with yourself since?

TESMAN.

Well, I and some of the others went home with one of the party, a jolly fellow, and took our morning coffee with him; or perhaps I should rather call it our night coffee—eh? But now, when I have rested a little, and given Eilert, poor fellow, time to have his sleep out, I must take this back to him.

HEDDA.

[*Holds out her hand for the packet.*] No—don't give it to him! Not in such a hurry, I mean. Let me read it first.

TESMAN.

No, my dearest Hedda, I mustn't, I really mustn't.

HEDDA.

You must not?

TESMAN.

No—for you can imagine what a state of despair he will be in when he wakens and misses the manuscript. He has no copy of it, you must know! He told me so.

HEDDA.

[*Looking searchingly at him.*] Can such a thing not be reproduced? Written over again?

TESMAN.

No, I don't think that would be possible. For the inspiration, you see——

HEDDA.

Yes, yes—I suppose it depends on that—— [*Lightly.*] But, by-the-bye—here is a letter for you.

TESMAN.

Fancy——!

HEDDA.

[*Handing it to him.*] It came early this morning.

TESMAN.

It's from Aunt Julia! What can it be? [*He lays the packet on the other footstool, opens the letter, runs his eye through it, and jumps up.*] Oh, Hedda—she says that poor Aunt Rina is dying!

HEDDA.

Well, we were prepared for that.

TESMAN.

And that if I want to see her again, I must make haste. I'll run in to them at once.

HEDDA.

[*Suppressing a smile.*] Will you run?

TESMAN.

Oh, my dearest Hedda—if you could only make up your mind to come with me! Just think!

HEDDA.

[*Rises and says wearily, repelling the idea.*] No,

no, don't ask me. I will not look upon sickness and death. I loathe all sorts of ugliness.

TESMAN.

Well, well, then——! [*Bustling around.*] My hat——? My overcoat——? Oh, in the hall——. I do hope I mayn't come too late, Hedda! Eh?

HEDDA.

Oh, if you run——

[BERTA *appears at the hall door.*

BERTA.

Judge Brack is at the door, and wishes to know if he may come in.

TESMAN.

At this time! No, I can't possibly see him.

HEDDA.

But I can. [*To* BERTA.] Ask Judge Brack to come in. [BERTA *goes out.*

HEDDA.

[*Quickly, whispering.*] The parcel, Tesman!

[*She snatches it up from the stool.*

TESMAN.

Yes, give it to me!

HEDDA.

No, no, I will keep it till you come back.

[*She goes to the writing-table and places it in the bookcase.* TESMAN *stands in a flurry of haste, and cannot get his gloves on.*

JUDGE BRACK *enters from the hall.*

HEDDA.

[*Nodding to him.*] You are an early bird, I must say.

BRACK.

Yes, don't you think so? [*To* TESMAN.] Are you on the move, too?

TESMAN.

Yes, I must rush off to my aunts'. Fancy—the invalid one is lying at death's door, poor creature.

BRACK.

Dear me, is she indeed? Then on no account let me detain you. At such a critical moment——

TESMAN.

Yes, I must really rush—— Good-bye! Good-bye! [*He hastens out by the hall door.*

HEDDA.

[*Approaching.*] You seem to have made a particularly lively night of it at your rooms, Judge Brack.

BRACK.

I assure you I have not had my clothes off, Mrs. Hedda.

HEDDA.

Not you, either?

BRACK.

No, as you may see. But what has Tesman been telling you of the night's adventures?

HEDDA.

Oh, some tiresome story. Only that they went and had coffee somewhere or other.

BRACK.

I have heard about that coffee-party already. Eilert Lövborg was not with them, I fancy?

HEDDA.

No, they had taken him home before that.

BRACK.

Tesman too?

HEDDA.

No, but some of the others, he said.

BRACK.

[*Smiling.*] George Tesman is really an ingenuous creature, Mrs. Hedda.

HEDDA.

Yes, heaven knows he is. Then is there something behind all this?

BRACK.

Yes, perhaps there may be.

HEDDA.

Well then, sit down, my dear Judge, and tell your story in comfort.

[*She seats herself to the left of the table.* BRACK *sits near her, at the long side of the table.*

HEDDA.

Now then?

BRACK.

I had special reasons for keeping track of my guests—or rather of some of my guests—last night.

HEDDA.

Of Eilert Lövborg among the rest, perhaps?

BRACK.

Frankly—yes.

HEDDA.

Now you make me really curious——

BRACK.

Do you know where he and one or two of the others finished the night, Mrs. Hedda?

HEDDA.

If it is not quite unmentionable, tell me.

BRACK.

Oh no, it's not at all unmentionable. Well, they put in an appearance at a particularly animated soirée.

HEDDA.

Of the lively kind?

BRACK.

Of the very liveliest——

HEDDA.

Tell me more of this, Judge Brack——

BRACK.

Lövborg, as well as the others, had been invited in advance. I knew all about it. But he had declined the invitation; for now, as you know, he has become a new man.

HEDDA.

Up at the Elvsteds', yes. But he went after all, then?

BRACK.

Well, you see, Mrs. Hedda—unhappily the spirit moved him at my rooms last evening——

HEDDA.

Yes, I hear he found inspiration.

BRACK.

Pretty violent inspiration. Well, I fancy that altered his purpose; for we menfolk are unfortunately not always so firm in our principles as we ought to be.

HEDDA.

Oh, I am sure you are an exception, Judge Brack. But as to Lövborg——?

BRACK.

To make a long story short—he landed at last in Mademoiselle Diana's rooms.

HEDDA.

Mademoiselle Diana's?

BRACK.

It was Mademoiselle Diana that was giving the soirée, to a select circle of her admirers and her lady friends.

HEDDA.

Is she a red-haired woman?

BRACK.

Precisely.

HEDDA.

A sort of a—singer?

BRACK.

Oh yes—in her leisure moments. And moreover a mighty huntress—of men—Mrs. Hedda. You have no doubt heard of her. Eilert Lövborg was one of her most enthusiastic protectors—in the days of his glory.

HEDDA.

And how did all this end?

BRACK.

Far from amicably, it appears. After a most tender meeting, they seem to have come to blows——

HEDDA.

Lövborg and she?

BRACK.

Yes. He accused her or her friends of having robbed him. He declared that his pocket-book had disappeared—and other things as well. In short, he seems to have made a furious disturbance.

HEDDA.

And what came of it all?

BRACK.

It came to a general scrimmage, in which the ladies as well as the gentlemen took part. Fortunately the police at last appeared on the scene.

HEDDA.

The police too?

BRACK.

Yes. I fancy it will prove a costly frolic for Eilert Lövborg, crazy being that he is.

HEDDA.

How so?

BRACK.

He seems to have made a violent resistance—to have hit one of the constables on the head and torn the coat off his back. So they had to march him off to the police-station with the rest.

HEDDA.

How have you learnt all this?

BRACK.

From the police themselves.

HEDDA.

[*Gazing straight before her.*] So that is what happened. Then he had no vine-leaves in his hair.

BRACK.

Vine-leaves, Mrs. Hedda?

HEDDA.

[*Changing her tone.*] But tell me now, Judge—what is your real reason for tracking out Eilert Lövborg's movements so carefully?

BRACK.

In the first place, it could not be entirely indifferent to me if it should appear in the police-court that he came straight from my house.

HEDDA.

Will the matter come into court then?

BRACK.

Of course. However, I should scarcely have troubled so much about that. But I thought that, as a friend of the family, it was my duty to supply you and Tesman with a full account of his nocturnal exploits.

HEDDA.

Why so, Judge Brack?

BRACK.

Why, because I have a shrewd suspicion that he intends to use you as a sort of blind.

HEDDA.

Oh, how can you think such a thing!

BRACK.

Good heavens, Mrs. Hedda—we have eyes in our head. Mark my words! This Mrs. Elvsted will be in no hurry to leave town again.

HEDDA.

Well, even if there should be anything between them, I suppose there are plenty of other places where they could meet.

BRACK.

Not a single home. Henceforth, as before, every respectable house will be closed against Eilert Lövborg.

HEDDA.

And so ought mine to be, you mean?

BRACK.

Yes. I confess it would be more than painful to me if this personage were to be made free of your house. How superfluous, how intrusive, he would be, if he were to force his way into——

HEDDA.

——into the triangle?

BRACK.

Precisely. It would simply mean that I should find myself homeless.

HEDDA.

[*Looks at him with a smile.*] So you want to be the one cock in the basket[1]—that is your aim.

BRACK.

[*Nods slowly and lowers his voice.*] Yes, that is my aim And for that I will fight—with every weapon I can command.

HEDDA.

[*Her smile vanishing.*] I see you are a dangerous person—when it comes to the point.

BRACK.

Do you think so?

HEDDA.

I am beginning to think so. And I am exceedingly glad to think—that you have no sort of hold over me.

[1] "Eneste hane i kurven"—a proverbial saying.

BRACK.

[*Laughing equivocally.*] Well well, Mrs. Hedda —perhaps you are right there. If I had, who knows what I might be capable of?

HEDDA.

Come come now, Judge Brack! That sounds almost like a threat.

BRACK.

[*Rising.*] Oh, not at all! The triangle, you know, ought, if possible, to be spontaneously constructed.

HEDDA.

There I agree with you.

BRACK.

Well, now I have said all I had to say; and I had better be getting back to town. Good-bye, Mrs. Hedda. [*He goes towards the glass door.*

HEDDA.

[*Rising.*] Are you going through the garden?

BRACK.

Yes, it's a short cut for me.

HEDDA.

And then it is a back way, too.

BRACK.

Quite so. I have no objection to back ways. They may be piquant enough at times.

HEDDA.

When there is ball practice going on, you mean?

BRACK.

[*In the doorway, laughing to her.*] Oh, people don't shoot their tame poultry, I fancy.

HEDDA.

[*Also laughing.*] Oh no, when there is only one cock in the basket——

[*They exchange laughing nods of farewell. He goes. She closes the door behind him.*

[HEDDA, *who has become quite serious, stands for a moment looking out. Presently she goes and peeps through the curtain over the middle doorway. Then she goes to the writing-table, takes* LÖVBORG'S *packet out of the bookcase, and is on the point of looking through its contents.* BERTA *is heard speaking loudly in the hall.* HEDDA *turns and listens. Then she hastily locks up the packet in the drawer, and lays the key on the inkstand.*

EILERT LÖVBORG, *with his greatcoat on and his hat in his hand, tears open the hall door. He looks somewhat confused and irritated.*

LÖVBORG.

[*Looking towards the hall.*] And I tell you I must and will come in! There!

[*He closes the door, turns, sees* HEDDA, *at once regains his self-control, and bows.*

HEDDA.

[*At the writing-table.*] Well, Mr. Lövborg, this is rather a late hour to call for Thea.

LÖVBORG.

You mean rather an early hour to call on you. Pray pardon me.

HEDDA.

How do you know that she is still here?

LÖVBORG.

They told me at her lodgings that she had been out all night.

HEDDA.

[*Going to the oval table.*] Did you notice anything about the people of the house when they said that?

LÖVBORG.

[*Looks inquiringly at her.*] Notice anything about them?

HEDDA.

I mean, did they seem to think it odd?

LÖVBORG.

[*Suddenly understanding.*] Oh yes, of course! I am dragging her down with me! However, I didn't notice anything.—I suppose Tesman is not up yet?

HEDDA.

No—I think not——

LÖVBORG.

When did he come home?

HEDDA.

Very late.

LÖVBORG.

Did he tell you anything?

HEDDA.

Yes, I gathered that you had had an exceedingly jolly evening at Judge Brack's.

LÖVBORG.

Nothing more?

HEDDA.

I don't think so. However, I was so dreadfully sleepy——

MRS. ELVSTED *enters through the curtains of the middle doorway.*

MRS. ELVSTED.

[*Going towards him.*] Ah, Lövborg! At last——!

LÖVBORG.

Yes, at last. And too late!

MRS. ELVSTED.

[*Looks anxiously at him.*] What is too late?

LÖVBORG.

Everything is too late now. It is all over with me.

MRS. ELVSTED.

Oh no, no—don't say that!

LÖVBORG.

You will say the same when you hear——

MRS. ELVSTED.

I won't hear anything!

HEDDA.

Perhaps you would prefer to talk to her alone? If so, I will leave you.

LÖVBORG.

No, stay—you too. I beg you to stay.

MRS. ELVSTED.

Yes, but I won't hear anything, I tell you.

LÖVBORG.

It is not last night's adventures that I want to talk about.

MRS. ELVSTED.

What is it then——?

LÖVBORG.

I want to say that now our ways must part.

MRS. ELVSTED.

Part!

HEDDA.

[*Involuntarily.*] I knew it!

LÖVBORG.

You can be of no more service to me, Thea.

MRS. ELVSTED.

How can you stand there and say that! No more service to you! Am I not to help you now, as before? Are we not to go on working together?

LÖVBORG.

Henceforward I shall do no work.

MRS. ELVSTED.

[*Despairingly.*] Then what am I to do with my life?

LÖVBORG.

You must try to live your life as if you had never known me.

MRS. ELVSTED.

But you know I cannot do that!

LÖVBORG.

Try if you cannot, Thea. You must go home again——

MRS. ELVSTED.

[*In vehement protest.*] Never in this world! Where you are, there will I be also! I will not let myself be driven away like this! I will remain here! I will be with you when the book appears.

HEDDA.

[*Half aloud, in suspense.*] Ah yes—the book!

LÖVBORG.

[*Looks at her.*] My book and Thea's; for that is what it is.

MRS. ELVSTED.

Yes, I feel that it is. And that is why I have a right to be with you when it appears! I will see with my own eyes how respect and honour pour in upon you afresh. And the happiness—the happiness—oh, I must share it with you!

LÖVBORG.

Thea—our book will never appear.

HEDDA.

Ah!

MRS. ELVSTED.

Never appear!

LÖVBORG.

Can never appear.

MRS. ELVSTED.

[*In agonised foreboding.*] Lövborg—what have you done with the manuscript?

HEDDA.

[*Looks anxiously at him.*] Yes, the manuscript——?

MRS. ELVSTED.

Where is it?

LÖVBORG.

Oh Thea—don't ask me about it!

MRS. ELVSTED.

Yes, yes, I will know. I demand to be told at once.

LÖVBORG.

The manuscript——. Well then—I have torn the manuscript into a thousand pieces.

MRS. ELVSTED.

[*Shrieks.*] Oh no, no——!

HEDDA.

[*Involuntarily.*] But that's not——

LÖVBORG.

[*Looks at her.*] Not true, you think?

HEDDA.

[*Collecting herself.*] Oh well, of course—since you say so. But it sounded so improbable——

LÖVBORG.

It is true, all the same.

MRS. ELVSTED.

[*Wringing her hands.*] Oh God—oh God, Hedda—torn his own work to pieces!

LÖVBORG.

I have torn my own life to pieces. So why should I not tear my life-work too——?

MRS. ELVSTED.

And you did this last night?

LÖVBORG.

Yes, I tell you! Tore it into a thousand pieces—and scattered them on the fiord—far out. There there is cool sea-water at any rate—let them drift upon it—drift with the current and the wind. And then presently they will sink—deeper and deeper—as I shall, Thea.

MRS. ELVSTED.

Do you know, Lövborg, that what you have done with the book—I shall think of it to my dying day as though you had killed a little child.

LÖVBORG.

Yes, you are right. It is a sort of child-murder.

MRS. ELVSTED.

How could you, then——! Did not the child belong to me too?

HEDDA.

[*Almost inaudibly.*] Ah, the child——

MRS. ELVSTED.

[*Breathing heavily.*] It is all over then. Well well, now I will go, Hedda.

HEDDA.

But you are not going away from town?

MRS. ELVSTED.

Oh, I don't know what I shall do. I see nothing but darkness before me.

[*She goes out by the hall door*

HEDDA.

[*Stands waiting for a moment.*] So you are not going to see her home, Mr. Lövborg?

LÖVBORG.

I? Through the streets? Would you have people see her walking with me?

HEDDA.

Of course I don't know what else may have happened last night. But is it so utterly irretrievable?

LÖVBORG.

It will not end with last night—I know that perfectly well. And the thing is that now I have no taste for that sort of life either. I won't begin it anew. She has broken my courage and my power of braving life out.

HEDDA.

[*Looking straight before her.*] So that pretty little fool has had her fingers in a man's destiny. [*Looks at him.*] But all the same, how could you treat her so heartlessly.

LÖVBORG.

Oh, don't say that it was heartless!

HEDDA.

To go and destroy what has filled her whole soul for months and years! You do not call that heartless!

LÖVBORG.

To you I can tell the truth, Hedda.

HEDDA.

The truth?

LÖVBORG.

First promise me—give me your word—that what I now confide to you Thea shall never know.

HEDDA.

I give you my word.

LÖVBORG.

Good. Then let me tell you that what I said just now was untrue.

HEDDA.

About the manuscript?

LÖVBORG.

Yes. I have not torn it to pieces—nor thrown it into the fiord.

HEDDA.

No, no——. But—where is it then?

LÖVBORG.

I have destroyed it none the less—utterly destroyed it, Hedda!

HEDDA.

I don't understand.

LÖVBORG.

Thea said that what I had done seemed to her like a child-murder.

HEDDA.

Yes, so she said.

LÖVBORG.

But to kill his child—that is not the worst thing a father can do to it.

HEDDA.

Not the worst?

LÖVBORG.

No. I wanted to spare Thea from hearing the worst.

HEDDA.

Then what is the worst?

LÖVBORG.

Suppose now, Hedda, that a man—in the small hours of the morning—came home to his child's mother after a night of riot and debauchery, and said: "Listen—I have been here and there—in this place and in that. And I have taken our child with me—to this place and to that. And I have lost the child—utterly lost it. The devil knows into what hands it may have fallen—who may have had their clutches on it."

HEDDA.

Well—but when all is said and done, you know —this was only a book——

LÖVBORG.

Thea's pure soul was in that book.

HEDDA.

Yes, so I understand.

LÖVBORG.

And you can understand, too, that for her and me together no future is possible.

HEDDA.

What path do you mean to take then?

LÖVBORG.

None. I will only try to make an end of it all—the sooner the better.

HEDDA.

[*A step nearer him.*] Eilert Lövborg—listen to me.—Will you not try to—to do it beautifully?

LÖVBORG.

Beautifully? [*Smiling.*] With vine-leaves in my hair, as you used to dream in the old days——?

HEDDA.

No, no. I have lost my faith in the the vine-leaves. But beautifully nevertheless! For once in a way!—Good-bye! You must go now—and do not come here any more.

LÖVBORG.

Good-bye, Mrs. Tesman. And give George Tesman my love. [*He is on the point of going.*

HEDDA.

No, wait! I must give you a memento to take with you.

[*She goes to the writing-table and opens the drawer and the pistol-case; then returns to* LÖVBORG *with one of the pistols.*

LÖVBORG.

[*Looks at her.*] This? Is this the memento?

HEDDA.

[*Nodding slowly.*] Do you recognise it? It was aimed at you once.

LÖVBORG.

You should have used it then.

HEDDA.

Take it—and do you use it now.

LÖVBORG.

[*Puts the pistol in his breast pocket.*] Thanks!

HEDDA.

And beautifully, Eilert Lövborg. Promise me that!

LÖVBORG.

Good-bye, Hedda Gabler.

[*He goes out by the hall door.*

[HEDDA *listens for a moment at the door. Then she goes up to the writing-table, takes out the packet of manuscript, peeps under the cover, draws a few of the sheets half out, and looks at them. Next she goes over and seats herself in the arm-chair beside the stove, with the packet in her lap. Presently she opens the stove door, and then the packet.*

HEDDA.

[*Throws one of the quires into the fire and whispers to herself.*] Now I am burning your child, Thea! —Burning it, curly-locks! [*Throwing one or two more quires into the stove.*] Your child and Eilert Lövborg's. [*Throws the rest in.*] I am burning— I am burning your child.

ACT FOURTH.

The same rooms at the TESMANS'. *It is evening. The drawing-room is in darkness. The back room is lighted by the hanging lamp over the table. The curtains over the glass door are drawn close.*

HEDDA, *dressed in black, walks to and fro in the dark room. Then she goes into the back room and disappears for a moment to the left. She is heard to strike a few chords on the piano. Presently she comes in sight again, and returns to the drawing-room.*

BERTA *enters from the right, through the inner room, with a lighted lamp, which she places on the table in front of the corner settee in the drawing-room. Her eyes are red with weeping, and she has black ribbons in her cap. She goes quietly and circumspectly out to the right.* HEDDA *goes up to the glass door, lifts the curtain a little aside, and looks out into the darkness.*

Shortly afterwards, MISS TESMAN, *in mourning, with a bonnet and veil on, comes in from the hall.* HEDDA *goes towards her and holds out her hand.*

MISS TESMAN.

Yes, Hedda, here I am, in mourning and forlorn; for now my poor sister has at last found peace.

HEDDA.

I have heard the news already, as you see. Tesman sent me a card.

MISS TESMAN.

Yes, he promised me he would. But nevertheless I thought that to Hedda—here in the house of life—I ought myself to bring the tidings of death.

HEDDA.

That was very kind of you.

MISS TESMAN.

Ah, Rina ought not to have left us just now. This is not the time for Hedda's house to be a house of mourning.

HEDDA.

[*Changing the subject.*] She died quite peacefully, did she not, Miss Tesman?

MISS TESMAN.

Oh, her end was so calm, so beautiful. And then she had the unspeakable happiness of seeing George once more—and bidding him good-bye.—Has he not come home yet?

HEDDA.

No. He wrote that he might be detained. But won't you sit down?

MISS TESMAN.

No thank you, my dear, dear Hedda. I should like to, but I have so much to do. I must prepare my dear one for her rest as well as I can. She shall go to her grave looking her best.

HEDDA.

Can I not help you in any way?

MISS TESMAN.

Oh, you must not think of it! Hedda Tesman must have no hand in such mournful work. Nor let her thoughts dwell on it either—not at this time.

HEDDA.

One is not always mistress of one's thoughts——

MISS TESMAN.

[*Continuing.*] Ah yes, it is the way of the world. At home we shall be sewing a shroud; and here there will soon be sewing too, I suppose—but of another sort, thank God!

GEORGE TESMAN *enters by the hall door.*

HEDDA.

Ah, you have come at last!

TESMAN.

You here, Aunt Julia? With Hedda? Fancy that!

MISS TESMAN.

I was just going, my dear boy. Well, have you done all you promised?

TESMAN.

No; I'm really afraid I have forgotten half of it. I must come to you again to-morrow. To-day my brain is all in a whirl. I can't keep my thoughts together.

MISS TESMAN.

Why, my dear George, you mustn't take it in this way.

TESMAN.

Mustn't——? How do you mean?

MISS TESMAN.

Even in your sorrow you must rejoice, as I do—rejoice that she is at rest.

TESMAN.

Oh yes, yes—you are thinking of Aunt Rina.

HEDDA.

You will feel lonely now, Miss Tesman.

MISS TESMAN.

Just at first, yes. But that will not last very long, I hope. I daresay I shall soon find an occupant for poor Rina's little room.

TESMAN.

Indeed? Who do you think will take it? Eh?

MISS TESMAN.

Oh, there's always some poor invalid or other in want of nursing, unfortunately.

HEDDA.

Would you really take such a burden upon you again?

MISS TESMAN.

A burden! Heaven forgive you, child—it has been no burden to me.

HEDDA.

But suppose you had a total stranger on your hands——

MISS TESMAN.

Oh, one soon makes friends with sick folk; and it's such an absolute necessity for me to have some one to live for. Well, heaven be praised, there may soon be something in this house, too, to keep an old aunt busy.

HEDDA.

Oh, don't trouble about anything here.

TESMAN.

Yes, just fancy what a nice time we three might have together, if——?

HEDDA.

If——?

TESMAN.

[*Uneasily.*] Oh, nothing. It will all come right. Let us hope so—eh?

MISS TESMAN.

Well well, I daresay you two want to talk to each other. [*Smiling.*] And perhaps Hedda may have something to tell you too, George. Good-bye! I must go home to Rina. [*Turning at the door.*] How strange it is to think that now Rina is with me and with my poor brother as well!

TESMAN.

Yes, fancy that, Aunt Julia! Eh?

[MISS TESMAN *goes out by the hall door.*

HEDDA.

[*Follows* TESMAN *coldly and searchingly with her eyes.*] I almost believe your Aunt Rina's death affects you more than it does your Aunt Julia.

TESMAN.

Oh, it's not that alone. It's Eilert I am so terribly uneasy about.

HEDDA.

[*Quickly.*] Is there anything new about him?

TESMAN.

I looked in at his rooms this afternoon, intending to tell him the manuscript was in safe keeping.

HEDDA.

Well, did you not find him?

TESMAN.

No. He wasn't at home. But afterwards I met Mrs. Elvsted, and she told me that he had been here early this morning.

HEDDA.

Yes, directly after you had gone.

TESMAN.

And he said that he had torn his manuscript to pieces—eh?

HEDDA.

Yes, so he declared.

TESMAN.

Why, good heavens, he must have been completely out of his mind! And I suppose you thought it best not to give it back to him, Hedda?

HEDDA.

No, he did not get it.

TESMAN.

But of course you told him that we had it?

HEDDA.

No. [*Quickly.*] Did you tell Mrs. Elvsted?

TESMAN.

No; I thought I had better not. But you ought to have told him. Fancy, if, in desperation, he should go and do himself some injury! Let me have the manuscript, Hedda! I will take it to him at once. Where is it?

HEDDA.

[*Cold and immovable, leaning on the arm-chair.*] I have not got it.

TESMAN.

Have not got it? What in the world do you mean?

HEDDA.

I have burnt it—every line of it.

TESMAN.

[*With a violent movement of terror.*] Burnt! Burnt Eilert's manuscript!

HEDDA.

Don't scream so. The servant might hear you.

TESMAN.

Burnt! Why, good God——! No, no, no! It's impossible!

HEDDA.

It is so, nevertheless.

TESMAN.

Do you know what you have done, Hedda? It's unlawful appropriation of lost property. Fancy that! Just ask Judge Brack, and he'll tell you what it is.

HEDDA.

I advise you not to speak of it—either to Judge Brack, or to any one else.

TESMAN.

But how could you do anything so unheard-of? What put it into your head? What possessed you? Answer me that—eh?

HEDDA.

[*Suppressing an almost imperceptible smile.*] I did it for your sake, George.

TESMAN.

For my sake!

HEDDA.

This morning, when you told me about what he had read to you——

TESMAN.

Yes yes—what then?

HEDDA.

You acknowledged that you envied him his work.

TESMAN.

Oh, of course I didn't mean that literally.

HEDDA.

No matter—I could not bear the idea that any one should throw you into the shade.

TESMAN.

[*In an outburst of mingled doubt and joy.*] Hedda! Oh, is this true? But—but—I never knew you show your love like that before. Fancy that!

HEDDA.

Well, I may as well tell you that—just at this time—— [*Impatiently, breaking off.*] No, no; you can ask Aunt Julia. She will tell you, fast enough.

TESMAN.

Oh, I almost think I understand you, Hedda! [*Clasps his hands together.*] Great heavens! do you really mean it! Eh?

HEDDA.

Don't shout so. The servant might hear.

TESMAN.

[*Laughing in irrepressible glee.*] The servant! Why, how absurd you are, Hedda. It's only my old Berta! Why, I'll tell Berta myself.

HEDDA.

[*Clenching her hands together in desperation.*] Oh, it is killing me,—it is killing me, all this!

TESMAN.

What is, Hedda? Eh?

HEDDA.

[*Coldly, controlling herself.*] All this—absurdity—George.

TESMAN.

Absurdity! Do you see anything absurd in my

being overjoyed at the news! But after all—perhaps I had better not say anything to Berta.

HEDDA.

Oh——why not that too?

TESMAN.

No, no, not yet! But I must certainly tell Aunt Julia. And then that you have begun to call me George too! Fancy that! Oh, Aunt Julia will be so happy—so happy!

HEDDA.

When she hears that I have burnt Eilert Lövborg's manuscript—for your sake?

TESMAN.

No, by-the-bye—that affair of the manuscript—of course nobody must know about that. But that you love me so much,[1] Hedda—Aunt Julia must really share my joy in that! I wonder, now, whether this sort of thing is usual in young wives? Eh?

HEDDA.

I think you had better ask Aunt Julia that question too.

TESMAN.

I will indeed, some time or other. [*Looks uneasy and downcast again.*] And yet the manuscript—the manuscript! Good God! it is terrible to think what will become of poor Eilert now.

[1] Literally, "That you burn for me."

MRS. ELVSTED, *dressed as in the first Act, with hat and cloak, enters by the hall door.*

MRS. ELVSTED.

[*Greets them hurriedly, and says in evident agitation.*] Oh, dear Hedda, forgive my coming again.

HEDDA.

What is the matter with you, Thea?

TESMAN.

Something about Eilert Lövborg again—eh?

MRS. ELVSTED.

Yes! I am dreadfully afraid some misfortune has happened to him.

HEDDA.

[*Seizes her arm.*] Ah,—do you think so!

TESMAN.

Why, good Lord—what makes you think that, Mrs. Elvsted?

MRS. ELVSTED.

I heard them talking of him at my boarding-house—just as I came in. Oh, the most incredible rumours are afloat about him to-day.

TESMAN.

Yes, fancy, so I heard too! And I can bear witness that he went straight home to bed last night. Fancy that!

HEDDA.

Well, what did they say at the boarding-house?

MRS. ELVSTED.

Oh, I couldn't make out anything clearly. Either they knew nothing definite, or else——. They stopped talking when they saw me; and I did not dare to ask.

TESMAN.

[*Moving about uneasily.*] We must hope—we must hope that you misunderstood them, Mrs. Elvsted.

MRS. ELVSTED.

No, no; I am sure it was of him they were talking. And I heard something about the hospital or——

TESMAN.

The hospital?

HEDDA.

No—surely that cannot be!

MRS. ELVSTED.

Oh, I was in such mortal terror! I went to his lodgings and asked for him there.

HEDDA.

You could make up your mind to that, Thea!

MRS. ELVSTED.

What else could I do? I really could bear the suspense no longer.

TESMAN.

But you didn't find him either—eh?

MRS. ELVSTED.

No. And the people knew nothing about him. He hadn't been home since yesterday afternoon, they said.

TESMAN.

Yesterday! Fancy, how could they say that?

MRS. ELVSTED.

Oh, I am sure something terrible must have happened to him.

TESMAN.

Hedda dear—how would it be if I were to go and make inquiries——?

HEDDA.

No, no—don't you mix yourself up in this affair.

JUDGE BRACK, *with his hat in his hand, enters by the hall door, which* BERTA *opens, and closes behind him. He looks grave and bows in silence.*

TESMAN.

Oh, is that you, my dear Judge? Eh?

BRACK.

Yes. It was imperative I should see you this evening.

TESMAN.

I can see you have heard the news about Aunt Rina?

BRACK.

Yes, that among other things.

TESMAN.

Isn't it sad—eh?

BRACK.

Well, my dear Tesman, that depends on how you look at it.

TESMAN.

[*Looks doubtfully at him.*] Has anything else happened?

BRACK.

Yes.

HEDDA.

[*In suspense.*] Anything sad, Judge Brack?

BRACK.

That, too, depends on how you look at it, Mrs. Tesman.

MRS. ELVSTED.

[*Unable to restrain her anxiety.*] Oh! it is something about Eilert Lövborg!

BRACK.

[*With a glance at her.*] What makes you think that, Madam? Perhaps you have already heard something——?

MRS. ELVSTED.

[*In confusion.*] No, nothing at all, but——

TESMAN.

Oh, for heaven's sake, tell us!

BRACK.

[*Shrugging his shoulders.*] Well, I regret to say Eilert Lövborg has been taken to the hospital. He is lying at the point of death.

MRS. ELVSTED.

[*Shrieks.*] Oh God! oh God——!

TESMAN.

To the hospital! And at the point of death

HEDDA.

[*Involuntarily.*] So soon then——

MRS. ELVSTED.

[*Wailing.*] And we parted in anger, Hedda!

HEDDA.

[*Whispers.*] Thea—Thea—be careful!

MRS. ELVSTED.

[*Not heeding her.*] I must go to him! I must see him alive!

BRACK.

It is useless, Madam. No one will be admitted.

MRS. ELVSTED.

Oh, at least tell me what has happened to him? What is it?

TESMAN.

You don't mean to say that he has himself—— Eh?

HEDDA.

Yes, I am sure he has.

TESMAN.

Hedda, how can you——?

BRACK.

[*Keeping his eyes fixed upon her.*] Unfortunately you have guessed quite correctly, Mrs. Tesman.

MRS. ELVSTED.

Oh, how horrible!

TESMAN.

Himself, then! Fancy that!

HEDDA.

Shot himself!

BRACK.

Rightly guessed again, Mrs. Tesman.

MRS. ELVSTED.

[*With an effort at self-control.*] When did it happen, Mr. Brack?

BRACK.

This afternoon—between three and four.

TESMAN.

But, good Lord, where did he do it? Eh?

BRACK.

[*With some hesitation.*] Where? Well—I suppose at his lodgings.

MRS. ELVSTED.

No, that cannot be; for I was there between six and seven.

BRACK.

Well then, somewhere else. I don't know exactly. I only know that he was found——. He had shot himself—in the breast.

MRS. ELVSTED.

Oh, how terrible! That he should die like that!

HEDDA.

[*To* BRACK.] Was it in the breast?

BRACK.

Yes—as I told you.

HEDDA.

Not in the temple?

BRACK.

In the breast, Mrs. Tesman.

HEDDA.

Well, well—the breast is a good place, too.

BRACK.

How do you mean, Mrs. Tesman?

HEDDA.

[*Evasively.*] Oh, nothing—nothing.

TESMAN.

And the wound is dangerous, you say—eh?

BRACK.

Absolutely mortal. The end has probably come by this time.

MRS. ELVSTED.

Yes, yes, I feel it. The end! The end! Oh, Hedda——!

TESMAN.

But tell me, how have you learnt all this?

BRACK.

[*Curtly.*] Through one of the police. A man I had some business with.

HEDDA.

[*In a clear voice.*] At last a deed worth doing!

TESMAN.

[*Terrified.*] Good heavens, Hedda! what are you saying?

HEDDA.

I say there is beauty in this.

BRACK.

H'm, Mrs. Tesman——

TESMAN.

Beauty! Fancy that!

MRS. ELVSTED.

Oh, Hedda, how can you talk of beauty in such an act!

HEDDA.

Eilert Lövborg has himself made up his account with life. He has had the courage to do—the one right thing.

MRS. ELVSTED.

No, you must never think that was how it happened! It must have been in delirium that he did it.

TESMAN.

In despair!

HEDDA.

That he did not. I am certain of that.

MRS. ELVSTED.

Yes, yes! In delirium! Just as when he tore up our manuscript.

BRACK.

[*Starting.*] The manuscript? Has he torn that up?

MRS. ELVSTED.

Yes, last night.

TESMAN.

[*Whispers softly.*] Oh, Hedda, we shall never get over this.

BRACK.

H'm, very extraordinary.

TESMAN.

[*Moving about the room.*] To think of Eilert going out of the world in this way! And not leaving behind him the book that would have immortalised his name——

MRS. ELVSTED.

Oh, if only it could be put together again!

TESMAN.

Yes, if it only could! I don't know what I would not give——

MRS. ELVSTED.

Perhaps it can, Mr. Tesman.

TESMAN.

What do you mean?

MRS. ELVSTED.

[*Searches in the pocket of her dress.*] Look here. I have kept all the loose notes he used to dictate from.

HEDDA.

[*A step forward.*] Ah——!

TESMAN.

You have kept them, Mrs. Elvsted! Eh?

MRS. ELVSTED.

Yes, I have them here. I put them in my pocket when I left home. Here they still are——

TESMAN.

Oh, do let me see them!

MRS. ELVSTED.

[*Hands him a bundle of papers.*] But they are in such disorder—all mixed up.

TESMAN.

Fancy, if we could make something out of them, after all! Perhaps if we two put our heads together——

MRS. ELVSTED.

Oh yes, at least let us try——

TESMAN.

We will manage it! We must! I will dedicate my life to this task.

HEDDA.

You, George? Your life?

TESMAN.

Yes, or rather all the time I can spare. My own collections must wait in the meantime. Hedda—you understand, eh? I owe this to Eilert's memory.

HEDDA.

Perhaps.

TESMAN.

And so, my dear Mrs. Elvsted, we will give our whole minds to it. There is no use in brooding over what can't be undone—eh? We must try to control our grief as much as possible, and——

MRS. ELVSTED.

Yes, yes, Mr. Tesman, I will do the best I can.

TESMAN.

Well then, come here. I can't rest until we have looked through the notes. Where shall we sit? Here? No, in there. in the back room. Excuse me, my dear Judge. Come with me, Mrs. Elvsted.

MRS. ELVSTED.

Oh, if only it were possible!

[TESMAN *and* MRS. ELVSTED *go into the back room. She takes off her hat and cloak. They both sit at the table under the hanging lamp, and are soon deep in an eager examination of the papers.* HEDDA *crosses to the stove and sits in the arm-chair. Presently* BRACK *goes up to her.*]

HEDDA.

[*In a low voice.*] Oh, what a sense of freedom it gives one, this act of Eilert Lövborg's.

BRACK.

Freedom, Mrs. Hedda? Well, of course, it is a release for him——

HEDDA.

I mean for me. It gives me a sense of freedom to know that a deed of deliberate courage is still possible in this world,—a deed of spontaneous beauty.

BRACK.

[*Smiling.*] H'm—my dear Mrs. Hedda——

HEDDA.

Oh, I know what you are going to say. For you are a kind of specialist too, like—you know!

BRACK.

[*Looking hard at her.*] Eilert Lövborg was more to you than perhaps you are willing to admit to yourself. Am I wrong?

HEDDA.

I don't answer such questions. I only know that Eilert Lövborg has had the courage to live his life after his own fashion. And then—the last great act, with its beauty! Ah! that he should have the will and the strength to turn away from the banquet of life—so early.

BRACK.

I am sorry, Mrs. Hedda,—but I fear I must dispel an amiable illusion.

HEDDA.

Illusion?

BRACK.

Which could not have lasted long in any case.

HEDDA.

What do you mean?

BRACK.

Eilert Lövborg did not shoot himself—voluntarily.

HEDDA.

Not voluntarily?

BRACK.

No. The thing did not happen exactly as I told it.

HEDDA.

[*In suspense.*] Have you concealed something? What is it?

BRACK.

For poor Mrs. Elvsted's sake I idealised the facts a little.

HEDDA.

What are the facts?

BRACK.

First, that he is already dead.

HEDDA.

At the hospital?

BRACK.

Yes—without regaining consciousness.

HEDDA.

What more have you concealed?

BRACK.

This—the event did not happen at his lodgings.

HEDDA.

Oh, that can make no difference.

BRACK.

Perhaps it may. For I must tell you—Eilert

Lövborg was found shot in—in Mademoiselle Diana's boudoir.

HEDDA.

[*Makes a motion as if to rise, but sinks back again.*] That is impossible, Judge Brack! He cannot have been there again to-day.

BRACK.

He was there this afternoon. He went there, he said, to demand the return of something which they had taken from him. Talked wildly about a lost child——

HEDDA.

Ah—so that was why——

BRACK.

I thought probably he meant his manuscript; but now I hear he destroyed that himself. So I suppose it must have been his pocket-book.

HEDDA.

Yes, no doubt. And there—there he was found?

BRACK.

Yes, there. With a pistol in his breast-pocket, discharged. The ball had lodged in a vital part.

HEDDA.

In the breast—yes.

BRACK.

No—in the bowels.

HEDDA.

[*Looks up at him with an expression of loathing.*] That too! Oh, what curse is it that makes everything I touch turn ludicrous and mean?

BRACK.

There is one point more, Mrs. Hedda—another disagreeable feature in the affair.

HEDDA.

And what is that?

BRACK.

The pistol he carried——

HEDDA.

[*Breathless.*] Well? What of it?

BRACK.

He must have stolen it.

HEDDA.

[*Leaps up.*] Stolen it! That is not true! He did not steal it!

BRACK.

No other explanation is possible. He must have stolen it——. Hush!

TESMAN *and* MRS. ELVSTED *have risen from the table in the back room, and come into the drawing-room.*

TESMAN.

[*With the papers in both his hands.*] Hedda dear, it is almost impossible to see under that lamp Think of that!

HEDDA.

Yes, I am thinking.

TESMAN.

Would you mind our sitting at your writing-table—eh?

HEDDA.

If you like. [*Quickly.*] No, wait! Let me clear it first!

TESMAN.

Oh, you needn't trouble, Hedda. There is plenty of room.

HEDDA.

No no, let me clear it, I say! I will take these things in and put them on the piano. There!

[*She has drawn out an object, covered with sheet music, from under the bookcase, places several other pieces of music upon it, and carries the whole into the inner room, to the left.* TESMAN *lays the scraps of paper on the writing-table, and moves the lamp there from the corner table. He and* MRS. ELVSTED *sit down and proceed with their work.* HEDDA *returns.*

HEDDA.

[*Behind* MRS. ELVSTED'S *chair, gently ruffling her hair.*] Well, my sweet Thea,—how goes it with Eilert Lövborg's monument?

MRS. ELVSTED.

[*Looks dispiritedly up at her.*] Oh, it will be terribly hard to put in order.

TESMAN.

We must manage it. I am determined. And arranging other people's papers is just the work for me.

[HEDDA *goes over to the stove, and seats herself on one of the footstools.* BRACK *stands over her, leaning on the arm-chair.*

HEDDA.

[*Whispers.*] What did you say about the pistol?

BRACK.

[*Softly.*] That he must have stolen it.

HEDDA.

Why stolen it?

BRACK.

Because every other explanation ought to be impossible, Mrs. Hedda.

HEDDA.

Indeed?

BRACK.

[*Glances at her.*] Of course Eilert Lövborg was here this morning. Was he not?

HEDDA.

Yes.

BRACK.

Were you alone with him?

HEDDA.

Part of the time.

BRACK.

Did you not leave the room whilst he was here?

HEDDA.

No.

BRACK.

Try to recollect. Were you not out of the room a moment?

HEDDA.

Yes, perhaps just a moment—out in the hall.

BRACK.

And where was your pistol-case during that time?

HEDDA.

I had it locked up in——

BRACK.

Well, Mrs. Hedda?

HEDDA.

The case stood there on the writing-table.

BRACK.

Have you looked since, to see whether both the pistols are there?

HEDDA.

No.

BRACK.

Well, you need not. I saw the pistol found in Lövborg's pocket, and I knew it at once as the one I had seen yesterday—and before, too.

HEDDA.

Have you it with you?

BRACK.

No; the police have it.

HEDDA.

What will the police do with it?

BRACK.

Search till they find the owner.

HEDDA.

Do you think they will succeed

BRACK.

[*Bends over her and whispers.*] No, Hedda Gabler—not so long as I say nothing.

HEDDA.

[*Looks frightened at him.*] And if you do not say nothing,—what then?

BRACK.

[*Shrugs his shoulders.*] There is always the possibility that the pistol was stolen.

HEDDA.

[*Firmly.*] Death rather than that.

BRACK.

[*Smiling.*] People say such things—but they don't do them.

HEDDA.

[*Without replying.*] And supposing the pistol was not stolen, and the owner is discovered? What then?

BRACK.

Well, Hedda—then comes the scandal.

HEDDA.

The scandal!

BRACK.

Yes, the scandal—of which you are so mortally afraid. You will, of course, be brought before the court—both you and Mademoiselle Diana. She will have to explain how the thing happened—whether it was an accidental shot or murder. Did the pistol go off as he was trying to take it out of his pocket, to threaten her with? Or did she tear the pistol out of his hand, shoot him, and push it back into his pocket? That would be quite like her; for she is an able-bodied young person, this same Mademoiselle Diana.

HEDDA.

But *I* have nothing to do with all this repulsive business.

BRACK.

No. But you will have to answer the question: Why did you give Eilert Lövborg the pistol? And what conclusions will people draw from the fact that you did give it to him?

HEDDA.

[*Lets her head sink.*] That is true. I did not think of that.

BRACK.

Well, fortunately, there is no danger, so long as I say nothing.

HEDDA.

[*Looks up at him.*] So I am in your power, Judge Brack. You have me at your beck and call, from this time forward.

BRACK.

[*Whispers softly.*] Dearest Hedda—believe me —I shall not abuse my advantage.

HEDDA.

I am in your power none the less. Subject to your will and your demands. A slave, a slave then! [*Rises impetuously.*] No, I cannot endure the thought of that! Never!

BRACK.

[*Looks half-mockingly at her.*] People generally get used to the inevitable.

HEDDA.

[*Returns his look.*] Yes, perhaps. [*She crosses to the writing-table. Suppressing an involuntary smile, she imitates* TESMAN'S *intonations.*] Well? Are you getting on, George? Eh?

TESMAN.

Heaven knows, dear. In any case it will be the work of months.

HEDDA.

[*As before.*] Fancy that! [*Passes her hands softly through* MRS. ELVSTED'S *hair.*] Doesn't it seem strange to you, Thea? Here are you sitting with Tesman—just as you used to sit with Eilert Lövborg?

MRS. ELVSTED.

Ah, if I could only inspire your husband in the same way!

HEDDA.

Oh, that will come too—in time.

TESMAN.

Yes, do you know, Hedda—I really think I begin to feel something of the sort. But won't you go and sit with Brack again?

HEDDA.

Is there nothing I can do to help you two?

TESMAN.

No, nothing in the world. [*Turning his head.*] I trust to you to keep Hedda company, my dear Brack!

BRACK.

[*With a glance at* HEDDA.] With the very greatest of pleasure.

HEDDA.

Thanks. But I am tired this evening. I will go in and lie down a little on the sofa.

TESMAN.

Yes, do dear—eh?

[HEDDA *goes into the back room and draws the curtains. A short pause. Suddenly she is heard playing a wild dance on the piano.*

MRS. ELVSTED.

[*Starts from her chair.*] Oh—what is that?

TESMAN.

[*Runs to the doorway.*] Why, my dearest Hedda—don't play dance-music to-night! Just think of Aunt Rina! And of Eilert too!

HEDDA.

[*Puts her head out between the curtains.*] And of Aunt Julia. And of all the rest of them.—After this, I will be quiet. [*Closes the curtains again.*]

TESMAN.

[*At the writing-table.*] It's not good for her to see us at this distressing work. I'll tell you what, Mrs. Elvsted,—you shall take the empty room at Aunt Julia's, and then I will come over in the evenings, and we can sit and work there—eh?

HEDDA.

[*In the inner room.*] I hear what you are saying, Tesman. But how am *I* to get through the evenings out here?

TESMAN.

[*Turning over the papers.*] Oh, I daresay Judge Brack will be so kind as to look in now and then, even though I am out.

BRACK.

[*In the arm-chair, calls out gaily.*] Every blessëd evening, with all the pleasure in life, Mrs. Tesman! We shall get on capitally together, we two!

HEDDA.

[*Speaking loud and clear.*] Yes, don't you flatter yourself we will, Judge Brack? Now that you are the one cock in the basket——

[*A shot is heard within.* TESMAN, MRS. ELVSTED, *and* BRACK *leap to their feet.*

TESMAN.

Oh, now she is playing with those pistols again.

[*He throws back the curtains and runs in, followed by* MRS. ELVSTED. HEDDA *lies stretched on the sofa, lifeless. Confusion and cries.* BERTA *enters in alarm from the right.*

TESMAN.

[*Shrieks to* BRACK.] Shot herself! Shot herself in the temple! Fancy that!

BRACK.

[*Half-fainting in the arm-chair.*] Good God! —people don't do such things

THE MASTER BUILDER

(1892)

CHARACTERS

HALVARD SOLNESS, *Master Builder.*

ALINE SOLNESS, *his wife.*

DOCTOR HERDAL, *physician.*

KNUT BROVIK, *formerly an architect, now in* SOLNESS'S *employment.*

RAGNAR BROVIK, *his son, draughtsman.*

KAIA FOSLI, *his niece, book-keeper.*

MISS HILDA WANGEL.

Some Ladies.

A Crowd in the street.

The action passes in and about SOLNESS'S *house.*

THE MASTER BUILDER.

PLAY IN THREE ACTS.

ACT FIRST.

A plainly-furnished work-room in the house of HALVARD SOLNESS. *Folding doors on the left lead out to the hall. On the right is the door leading to the inner rooms of the house. At the back is an open door into the draughtsmen's office. In front, on the left, a desk with books, papers and writing materials. Further back than the folding door, a stove. In the right-hand corner, a sofa, a table, and one or two chairs. On the table a water-bottle and glass. A smaller table, with a rocking-chair and arm-chair, in front on the right. Lighted lamps, with shades, on the table in the draughtsmen's office, on the table in the corner, and on the desk.*

In the draughtsmen's office sit KNUT BROVIK *and his son* RAGNAR, *occupied with plans and calculations. At the desk in the outer office stands* KAIA FOSLI, *writing in the ledger.* KNUT BROVICK *is a spare old man with white hair and beard. He wears a rather threadbare but well-brushed black coat, spectacles, and a somewhat discoloured white neckcloth.* RAGNAR BROVIK *is a well-dressed, light-haired man in his thirties, with a slight stoop.* KAIA FOSLI *is a slightly built girl, a little over twenty, carefully dressed, and delicate-looking. She has a green shade over her eyes.—All three go on working for some time in silence.*

KNUT BROVIK.

[*Rises suddenly, as if in distress, from the table; breathes heavily and laboriously as he comes forward into the doorway.*] No, I can't bear it much longer!

KAIA.

[*Going up to him.*] You are feeling very ill this evening, are you not, uncle?

BROVIK.

Oh, I seem to get worse every day.

RAGNAR.

[*Has risen and advances.*] You ought to go home, father. Try to get a little sleep——

BROVIK.

[*Impatiently.*] Go to bed, I suppose? Would you have me stifled outright?

KAIA.

Then take a little walk.

RAGNAR.

Yes, do. I will come with you.

BROVIK.

[*With warmth.*] I will not go till he comes! I

am determined to have it out this evening with —[*in a tone of suppressed bitterness*]—with him—with the chief.

KAIA.

[*Anxiously.*] Oh no, uncle,—do wait awhile before doing that!

RAGNAR.

Yes, better wait, father!

BROVIK.

[*Draws his breath laboriously.*] Ha—ha—! *I* haven't much time for waiting.

KAIA.

[*Listening.*] Hush! I hear him on the stairs.

[*All three go back to their work. A short silence.*

HALVARD SOLNESS *comes in through the hall door. He is a man no longer young, but healthy and vigorous, with close-cut curly hair, dark moustache and dark thick eyebrows. He wears a greyish-green buttoned jacket with an upstanding collar and broad lappels. On his head he wears a soft grey felt hat, and he has one or two light portfolios under his arm.*

SOLNESS.

[*Near the door, points towards the draughtsmen's office, and asks in a whisper:*] Are they gone?

KAIA.

[*Softly, shaking her head.*] No.

[*She takes the shade off her eyes.* SOLNESS *crosses the room, throws his hat on a chair, places the portfolios on the table by the sofa, and approaches the desk again.* KAIA *goes on writing without intermission, but seems nervous and uneasy.*

SOLNESS.

[*Aloud.*] What is that you are entering, Miss Fosli?

KAIA.

[*Starts.*] Oh, it is only something that——

SOLNESS.

Let me look at it, Miss Fosli. [*Bends over her, pretends to be looking into the ledger, and whispers:*] Kaia!

KAIA.

[*Softly, still writing.*] Well?

SOLNESS.

Why do you always take that shade off when I come?

KAIA.

[*As before.*] I look so ugly with it on.

SOLNESS.

[*Smiling.*] Then you don't like to look ugly, Kaia?

KAIA.

[*Half glancing up at him.*] Not for all the world. Not in your eyes.

SOLNESS.

[*Strokes her hair gently.*] Poor, poor little Kaia——

KAIA.

[*Bending her head.*] Hush—they can hear you!

[SOLNESS *strolls across the room to the right, turns and pauses at the door of the draughtsmen's office.*

SOLNESS.

Has any one been here for me?

RAGNAR.

[*Rising.*] Yes, the young couple who want a villa built, out at Lövstrand.

SOLNESS.

[*Growling.*] Oh, those two! They must wait. I am not quite clear about the plans yet.

RAGNAR.

[*Advancing, with some hesitation.*] They were very anxious to have the drawings at once.

SOLNESS.

[*As before.*] Yes, of course—so they all are.

BROVIK.

[*Looks up.*] They say they are longing so to get into a house of their own.

SOLNESS.

Yes, yes—we know all that! And so they are content to take whatever is offered them. They get a—a roof over their heads—an address—but nothing to call a home. No thank you! In that case, let them apply to somebody else. Tell them that, the next time they call.

BROVIK.

[*Pushes his glasses up on to his forehead and looks in astonishment at him.*] To somebody else? Are you prepared to give up the commission?

SOLNESS.

[*Impatiently.*] Yes, yes, yes, devil take it! If that is to be the way of it——. Rather that, than build away at random. [*Vehemently.*] Besides, I know very little about these people as yet.

BROVIK.

The people are safe enough. Ragnar knows them. He is a friend of the family. Perfectly safe people.

SOLNESS.

Oh, safe—safe enough! That is not at all what I mean. Good lord—don't you understand me either? [*Angrily.*] I won't have anything to do with these strangers. They may apply to whom they please, so far as I am concerned.

BROVIK.

[*Rising.*] Do you really mean that?

SOLNESS.

[*Sulkily.*] Yes I do.—For once in a way.

[*He comes forward.*

[BROVIK *exchanges a glance with* RAGNAR, *who makes a warning gesture. Then* BROVIK *comes into the front room.*

BROVIK.

May I have a few words with you?

SOLNESS.

Certainly.

BROVIK.

[*To* KAIA.] Just go in there for a moment, Kaia.

KAIA.

[*Uneasily.*] Oh, but uncle——

BROVIK.

Do as I say, child. And shut the door after you.

[KAIA *goes reluctantly into the draughtsmen's office, glances anxiously and imploringly at* SOLNESS, *and shuts the door.*

BROVIK.

[*Lowering his voice a little.*] I don't want the poor children to know how ill I am.

SOLNESS.

Yes, you have been looking very poorly of late.

BROVIK.

It will soon be all over with me. My strength is ebbing—from day to day.

SOLNESS.

Won't you sit down?

BROVIK.

Thanks—may I?

SOLNESS.

[*Placing the arm-chair more conveniently.*] Here—take this chair.—And now?

BROVIK.

[*Has seated himself with difficulty.*] Well, you see, it's about Ragnar. That is what weighs most upon me. What is to become of him?

SOLNESS.

Of course your son will stay with me as long as ever he likes.

BROVIK.

But that is just what he does not like. He feels that he cannot stay here any longer.

SOLNESS.

Why, I should say he was very well off here. But if he wants more money, I should not mind——

BROVIK.

No, no! It is not that. [*Impatiently.*] But sooner or later he, too, must have a chance of doing something on his own account.

SOLNESS.

[*Without looking at him.*] Do you think that Ragnar has quite talent enough to stand alone?

BROVIK.

No, that is just the heartbreaking part of it—I have begun to have my doubts about the boy. For you have never said so much as—as one encouraging word about him. And yet I cannot but think there must be something in him—he can't be without talent.

SOLNESS.

Well, but he has learnt nothing—nothing thoroughly, I mean. Except, of course, to draw.

BROVIK.

[*Looks at him with covert hatred, and says hoarsely.*] You had learned little enough of the business when you were in my employment. But that did not prevent you from setting to work—[*breathing with difficulty*]—and pushing your way up, and taking the wind out of my sails—mine, and so many other people's.

SOLNESS.

Yes, you see—circumstances favoured me.

BROVIK.

You are right there. Everything favoured you. But then how can you have the heart to let me go to my grave—without having seen what Ragnar is fit for? And of course I am anxious to see them married, too—before I go.

SOLNESS.

[*Sharply.*] Is it she who wishes it?

BROVIK.

Not Kaia so much as Ragnar—he talks about it every day. [*Appealingly.*] You must—you *must* help him to get some independent work now! I *must* see something that the lad has done. Do you hear?

SOLNESS.

[*Peevishly.*] Hang it, man, you can't expect me to drag commissions down from the moon for him!

BPOVIK.

He has the chance of a capital commission at this very moment. A big bit of work.

SOLNESS.

[*Uneasily, startled.*] Has he?

BROVIK.

If you would give your consent.

SOLNESS.

What sort of work do you mean?

BROVIK.

[*With some hesitation.*] He can have the building of that villa out at Lövstrand.

SOLNESS.

That! Why I am going to build that myself.

BROVIK.

Oh you don't much care about doing it.

SOLNESS.

[*Flaring up.*] Don't care! I! Who dares to say that?

BROVIK.

You said so yourself just now.

SOLNESS.

Oh, never mind what I say.—Would they give Ragnar the building of that villa?

BROVIK.

Yes. You see, he knows the family. And then —just for the fun of the thing—he has made drawings and estimates and so forth——

SOLNESS.

Are they pleased with the drawings? The people who will have to live in the house?

BROVIK.

Yes. If you would only look through them and approve of them——

SOLNESS.

Then they would let Ragnar build their home for them?

BROVIK.

They were immensely pleased with his idea. They thought it exceedingly original, they said.

SOLNESS.

Oho! Original! Not the old-fashioned stuff that *I* am in the habit of turning out!

BROVIK.

It seemed to them different.

SOLNESS.

[*With suppressed irritation.*] So it was to see Ragnar that they came here—whilst I was out!

BROVIK.

They came to call upon you—and at the same time to ask whether you would mind retiring——

SOLNESS.

[*Angrily.*] Retire? I?

BROVIK.

In case you thought that Ragnar's drawings——

SOLNESS.

I! Retire in favour of your son!

BROVIK.

Retire from the agreement, they meant.

SOLNESS.

Oh, it comes to the same thing. [*Laughs angrily.*] So that is it, is it? Halvard Solness is to see about retiring now! To make room for younger men! For the very youngest, perhaps! He must make room! Room! Room!

BROVIK.

Why, good heavens! there is surely room for more than one single man——

SOLNESS.

Oh, there's not so very much room to spare either. But, be that as it may—I will never retire! I will never give way to anybody! Never of my own free will. Never in this world will I do that!

BROVIK.

[*Rises with difficulty.*] Then I am to pass out of life without any certainty? Without a gleam of happiness? Without any faith or trust in Ragnar? Without having seen a single piece of work of his doing? Is that to be the way of it?

SOLNESS.

[*Turns half aside, and mutters.*] H'm—don't ask more just now.

BROVIK.

I must have an answer to this one question. Am I to pass out of life in such utter poverty?

SOLNESS.

[*Seems to struggle with himself; finally he says, in a low but firm voice:*] You must pass out of life as best you can.

BROVIK.

Then be it so. [*He goes up the room.*

SOLNESS.

[*Following him, half in desperation.*] Don't you understand that I cannot help it? I am what I am, and I cannot change my nature!

BROVIK.

No, on; I suppose you can't. [*Reels and supports himself against the sofa-table.*] May I have a glass of water?

SOLNESS.

By all means. [*Fills a glass and hands it to him.*

BROVIK.

Thanks. [*Drinks and puts the glass down again.*
[SOLNESS *goes up and opens the door of the draughtsmen's office.*

SOLNESS.

Ragnar—you must come and take your father home.

RAGNAR *rises quickly. He and* KAIA *come into the work-room.*

RAGNAR.

What is the matter, father?

BROVIK.

Give me your arm. Now let us go.

RAGNAR.

Very well. You had better put your things on, too, Kaia.

SOLNESS.

Miss Fosli must stay—just for a moment. There is a letter I want written.

BROVIK.

[*Looks at* SOLNESS.] Good night. Sleep well—if you can.

SOLNESS.

Good night.

[BROVIK *and* RAGNAR *go out by the hall-door.* KAIA *goes to the desk.* SOLNESS *stands with bent head, to the right, by the arm-chair.*

KAIA.

[*Dubiously.*] Is there any letter——?

SOLNESS.

[*Curtly.*] No, of course not. [*Looks sternly at her.*] Kaia!

KAIA.

[*Anxiously, in a low voice.*] Yes!

SOLNESS.

[*Points imperatively to a spot on the floor.*] Come here! At once!

KAIA.

[*Hesitatingly.*] Yes.

SOLNESS.

[*As before.*] Nearer!

KAIA.

[*Obeying.*] What do you want with me?

SOLNESS.

[*Looks at her for a while.*] Is it you I have to thank for all this?

KAIA.

No, no, don't think that!

SOLNESS.

But confess now—you want to get married!

KAIA.

[*Softly.*] Ragnar and I have been engaged for four or five years, and so——

SOLNESS.

And so you think it time there were an end of it. Is not that so?

KAIA.

Ragnar and Uncle say I *must*. So I suppose I shall have to give in.

SOLNESS.

[*More gently.*] Kaia, don't you really care a little bit for Ragnar, too?

KAIA.

I cared very much for Ragnar once—before I came here to you.

SOLNESS.

But you don't now? Not in the least?

KAIA.

[*Passionately, clasping her hands and holding them out towards him.*] Oh, you know very well there is only one person I care for now! One, and one only, in all the world! I shall never care for any one else.

SOLNESS.

Yes, you say that. And yet you go away from me—leave me alone here with everything on my hands.

KAIA.

But could I not stay with you, even if Ragnar——?

SOLNESS.

[*Repudiating the idea.*] No, no, that is quite impossible. If Ragnar leaves me and starts work on his own account, then of course he will need you himself.

KAIA.

[*Wringing her hands.*] Oh, I feel as if I could not be separated from you! It's quite, quite impossible!

SOLNESS.

Then be sure you get those foolish notions out of Ragnar's head. Marry him as much as you please—[*Alters his tone.*] I mean—don't let him throw up his good situation with me. For then I can keep you too, my dear Kaia.

KAIA.

Oh yes, how lovely that would be, if it could only be managed!

SOLNESS.

[*Clasps her head with with his two hands and whispers.*] For I cannot get on without you, you see. I must have you with me every single day.

KAIA.

[*In nervous exaltation.*]. My God! My God!

SOLNESS.

[*Kisses her hair.*] Kaia—Kaia!

KAIA.

[*Sinks down before him.*] Oh, how good you are to me! How unspeakably good you are!

SOLNESS.

[*Vehemently.*] Get up! For goodness' sake get up! I think I hear some one!

[*He helps her to rise. She staggers over to the desk.*

MRS. SOLNESS *enters by the door on the right. She looks thin and wasted with grief, but shows traces of bygone beauty. Blonde ringlets. Dresseed with good taste, wholly in black. Speaks somewhat slowly and in a plaintive voice.*

MRS. SOLNESS.

[*In the doorway.*] Halvard!

SOLNESS.

[*Turns.*] Oh, are you there, my dear——?

MRS. SOLNESS.

[*With a glance at* KAIA.] I am afraid I am disturbing you.

SOLNESS.

Not in the least. Miss Fosli has only a short letter to write.

MRS. SOLNESS.

Yes, so I see.

SOLNESS.

What do you want with me, Aline?

MRS. SOLNESS.

I merely wanted to tell you that Dr. Herdal is in the drawing-room. Won't you come and see him, Halvard?

SOLNESS.

[*Looks suspiciously at her.*] H'm—is the doctor so very anxious to talk to me?

MRS. SOLNESS.

Well, not exactly anxious. He really came to see me; but he would like to say how-do-you-do to you at the same time.

SOLNESS.

[*Laughs to himself.*] Yes, I daresay. Well, you must ask him to wait a little.

MRS. SOLNESS.

Then you will come in presently?

SOLNESS.

Perhaps I will. Presently, presently, dear. In a little while.

MRS. SOLNESS.

[*Glancing again at* KAIA.] Well now, don't forget, Halvard.

[*Withdraws and closes the door behind her.*

KAIA.

[*Softly.*] Oh dear, oh dear—I am sure Mrs. Solness thinks ill of me in some way!

SOLNESS.

Oh, not in the least. Not more than usual at any rate. But all the same, you had better go now, Kaia.

KAIA.

Yes, yes, now I must go.

SOLNESS.

[*Severely.*] And mind you get that matter settled for me. Do you hear?

KAIA.

Oh, if it only depended on me——

SOLNESS.

I will have it settled, I say! And to-morrow too—not a day later!

KAIA.

[*Terrified.*] If there's nothing else for it, I am quite willing to break off the engagement.

SOLNESS.

[*Angrily.*] Break it off. Are you mad? Would you think of breaking it off?

KAIA.

[*Distracted.*] Yes, if necessary. For I must—I must stay here with you! I can't leave you! That is utterly—utterly impossible!

SOLNESS.

[*With a sudden outburst.*] But deuce take it—how about Ragnar then! It's Ragnar that I——

KAIA.

[*Looks at him with terrified eyes.*] It is chiefly on Ragnar's account, that—that you——?

SOLNESS.

[*Collecting himself.*] No, no, of course not! You don't understand me either. [*Gently and softly.*] Of course it is you I want to keep—you above everything, Kaia. But for that very reason, you must prevent Ragnar, too, from throwing up his situation. There, there,—now go home.

KAIA.

Yes, yes—good-night, then.

SOLNESS.

Good night. [*As she is going.*] Oh, stop a moment! Are Ragnar's drawings in there?

KAIA.

I did not see him take them with him.

SOLNESS.

Then just go and find them for me. I might perhaps glance over them, after all.

KAIA.

[*Happy.*] Oh yes, please do!

SOLNESS.

For your sake, Kaia dear. Now, let me have them at once, please.

[KAIA *hurries into the draughtsmen's office, searches anxiously in the table-drawer, finds a portfolio and brings it with her.*

KAIA.

Here are all the drawings.

SOLNESS.

Good. Put them down there on the table.

KAIA.

[*Putting down the portfolio.*] Good night, then. [*Beseechingly.*] And please, please think kindly of me.

SOLNESS.

Oh, that I always do. Good-night, my dear little Kaia. [*Glances to the right.*] Go, go now!

MRS. SOLNESS *and* DR. HERDAL *enter by the door on the right. He is a stoutish, elderly man, with a round, good-humoured face, clean shaven, with thin, light hair, and gold spectacles.*

MRS. SOLNESS.

[*Still in the doorway.*] Halvard, I cannot keep the doctor any longer.

SOLNESS.

Well then, come in here.

MRS. SOLNESS.

[*To* KAIA, *who is turning down the desk-lamp.*] Have you finished the letter already, Miss Fosli?

KAIA.

[*In confusion.*] The letter——?

SOLNESS.

Yes, it was quite a short one.

MRS. SOLNESS.

It must have been very short.

SOLNESS.

You may go now, Miss Fosli. And please come in good time to-morrow morning.

KAIA.

I will be sure to. Good-night, Mrs. Solness.
[*She goes out by the hall door.*

MRS. SOLNESS.

She must be quite an acquisition to you, Halvard, this Miss Fosli.

SOLNESS.

Yes, indeed. She is useful in all sorts of ways.

MRS. SOLNESS.

So it seems.

DR. HERDAL.

Is she good at book-keeping too?

SOLNESS.

Well—of course she has had a good deal of practice during these two years. And then she is so nice and willing to do whatever one asks of her.

MRS. SOLNESS.

Yes, that must be very delightful——

SOLNESS.

It is. Especially when one is not too much accustomed to that sort of thing.

MRS. SOLNESS.

[*In a tone of gentle remonstrance.*] Can you say that, Halvard?

SOLNESS.

Oh, no, no, my dear Aline; I beg your pardon.

MRS. SOLNESS.

There's no occasion.—Well then, doctor, you will come back later on, and have a cup of tea with us?

DR. HERDAL.

I have only that one patient to see, and then I'll come back.

MRS. SOLNESS.

Thank you.

[*She goes out by the door on the right.*

SOLNESS.

Are you in a hurry, doctor?

DR. HERDAL.

No, not at all.

SOLNESS.

May I have a little chat with you?

DR. HERDAL.

With the greatest of pleasure.

SOLNESS.

Then let us sit down. [*He motions the doctor to take the rocking-chair, and sits down himself in the arm-chair. Looks searchingly at him.*] Tell me—did you notice anything odd about Aline?

DR. HERDAL.

Do you mean just now, when she was here?

SOLNESS.

Yes, in her manner to me. Did you notice anything?

DR. HERDAL.

[*Smiling.*] Well, I admit—one couldn't well avoid noticing that your wife—h'm——

SOLNESS.

Well?

DR. HERDAL.

—that your wife is not particularly fond of this Miss Fosli.

SOLNESS.

Is that all? I have noticed that myself.

DR. HERDAL.

And I must say I am scarcely surprised at it.

SOLNESS.

At what?

DR. HERDAL.

That she should not exactly approve of your seeing so much of another woman, all day and every day.

SOLNESS.

No, no, I suppose you are right there—and Aline too. But it's impossible to make any change.

DR. HERDAL.

Could you not engage a clerk?

SOLNESS.

The first man that came to hand? No, thank you—that would never do for me.

DR. HERDAL.

But now, if your wife——? Suppose, with her delicate health, all this tries her too much?

SOLNESS.

Even then—I might almost say—it can make no difference. I must keep Kaia Fosli. No one else could fill her place.

DR. HERDAL.

No one else?

SOLNESS.

[*Curtly.*] No, no one.

DR. HERDAL.

[*Drawing his chair closer.*] Now listen to me, my dear Mr. Solness. May I ask you a question, quite between ourselves?

SOLNESS.

By all means.

DR. HERDAL.

Women, you see—in certain matters, they have a deucedly keen intuition——

SOLNESS.

They have, indeed. There is not the least doubt of that. But——?

DR. HERDAL.

Well, tell me now—if your wife can't endure this Kaia Fosli——?

SOLNESS.

Well, what then?

DR. HERDAL.

—may she not have just—just the least little bit of reason for this instinctive dislike?

SOLNESS.

[*Looks at him and rises.*] Oho!

DR. HERDAL.

Now don't be offended—but hasn't she?

SOLNESS.

[*With curt decision.*] No.

DR. HERDAL.

No reason of any sort?

SOLNESS.

No other reason than her own suspicious nature.

DR. HERDAL.

I know you have known a good many women in your time.

SOLNESS.

Yes, I have.

DR. HERDAL.

And have been a good deal taken with some of them, too.

SOLNESS.

Oh yes, I don't deny it.

DR. HERDAL.

But as regards Miss Fosli, then? There is nothing of that sort in the case?

SOLNESS.

No; nothing at all—on my side.

DR. HERDAL.

But on her side?

SOLNESS.

I don't think you have any right to ask that question, doctor.

DR. HERDAL.

Well, you know, we were discussing your wife's intuition.

SOLNESS.

So we were. And for that matter—[*lowers his voice*]—Aline's intuition, as you call it—in a certain sense, it has not been so far astray.

DR. HERDAL.

Aha! there we have it!

SOLNESS.

[*Sits down.*] Doctor Herdal—I am going to tell you a strange story—if you care to listen to it.

DR. HERDAL.

I like listening to strange stories.

SOLNESS.

Very well then. I daresay you recollect that I took Knut Brovik and his son into my employment—after the old man's business had gone to the dogs

DR. HERDAL.

Yes, so I have understood.

SOLNESS.

You see, they really are clever fellows, these two. Each of them has talent in his own way. But then the son took it into his head to get engaged; and the next thing, of course, was that he wanted to get married—and begin to build on his own account. That is the way with all these young people.

DR. HERDAL.

[*Laughing.*] Yes, they have a bad habit of wanting to marry.

SOLNESS.

Just so. But of course that did not suit my plans; for I needed Ragnar myself—and the old man too. He is exceedingly good at calculating bearing-strains and cubic contents—and all that sort of devilry, you know.

DR. HERDAL.

Oh yes, no doubt that's indispensable.

SOLNESS.

Yes, it is. But Ragnar was absolutely bent on setting to work for himself. He would hear of nothing else.

DR. HERDAL.

But he has stayed with you all the same.

SOLNESS.

Yes, I'll tell you how that came about. One day this girl, Kaia Fosli, came to see them on some errand or other. She had never been here before. And when I saw how utterly infatuated they were with each other, the thought occurred to me: if I could only get her into the office here, then perhaps Ragnar too would stay where he is.

DR. HERDAL.

That was not at all a bad idea.

SOLNESS.

Yes, but at the time I did not breathe a word of what was in my mind. I merely stood and looked at her—and kept on wishing intently that I could have her here. Then I talked to her a little, in a friendly way—about one thing and another. And then she went away.

DR. HERDAL.

Well?

SOLNESS.

Well then, next day, pretty late in the evening, when old Brovik and Ragnar had gone home, she came here again, and behaved as if I had made an arrangement with her.

DR. HERDAL.

An arrangement? What about?

SOLNESS.

About the very thing my mind had been fixed on. But I hadn't said one single word about it.

DR. HERDAL.

That was most extraordinary.

SOLNESS.

Yes, was it not? And now she wanted to know what she was to do here—whether she could begin the very next morning, and so forth.

DR. HERDAL.

Don't you think she did it in order to be with her sweetheart?

SOLNESS.

That was what occurred to me at first. But no, that was not it. She seemed to drift quite away from him—when once she had come here to me.

DR. HERDAL.

She drifted over to you, then?

SOLNESS.

Yes, entirely. If I happen to look at her when her back is turned, I can tell that she feels it. She quivers and trembles the moment I come near her. What do you think of *that*?

DR. HERDAL.

H'm—that's not very hard to explain.

SOLNESS.

Well, but what about the other thing? That she believed I had said to her what I had only wished and willed—silently—inwardly—to myself? What do you say to *that*? Can you explain that, Dr. Herdal?

DR. HERDAL.

No, I won't undertake to do that.

SOLNESS.

I felt sure you would not; and so I have never cared to talk about it till now.—But it's a cursed nuisance to me in the long run, you understand. Here have I got to go on day after day pretending——. And it's a shame to treat her so, too, poor girl. [*Vehemently.*] But I *cannot* do anything else. For if *she* runs away from me—then Ragnar will be off too.

DR. HERDAL.

And you have not told your wife the rights of the story?

SOLNESS.

No.

DR. HERDAL.

Then why on earth don't you?

SOLNESS.

[*Looks fixedly at him, and says in a low voice:*] Because I seem to find a sort of—of salutary self-torture in allowing Aline to do me an injustice.

DR. HERDAL.

[*Shakes his head.*] I don't in the least understand what you mean.

SOLNESS.

Well, you see—it is like paying off a little bit of a huge, immeasurable debt——

DR. HERDAL.

To your wife?

SOLNESS.

Yes; and that always helps to relieve one's mind a little. One can breathe more freely for a while, you understand.

DR. HERDAL.

No, goodness knows, I don't understand at all——

SOLNESS.

[*Breaking off, rises again.*] Well, well, well—then we won't talk any more about it. [*He saunters across the room, returns, and stops beside the table. Looks at the doctor with a sly smile.*] I suppose you think you have drawn me out nicely now, doctor?

DR. HERDAL.

[*With some irritation.*] Drawn you out? Again I have not the faintest notion what you mean, Mr. Solness.

SOLNESS.

Oh come, out with it; I have seen it quite clearly, you know.

DR. HERDAL.

What have you seen?

SOLNESS.

[*In a low voice, slowly.*] That you have been quietly keeping an eye upon me.

DR. HERDAL.

That *I* have! And why in all the world should I do that?

SOLNESS.

Because you think that I—— [*Passionately.*] Well, devil take it—you think the same of me as Aline does.

DR. HERDAL.

And what does she think about you?

SOLNESS.

[*Having recovered his self-control.*] She has begun to think that I am—that I am—ill.

DR. HERDAL.

Ill! You! She has never hinted such a thing to me. Why, what can she think is the matter with you?

SOLNESS.

[*Leans over the back of the chair and whispers.*] Aline has made up her mind that I am mad. That is what she thinks.

DR. HERDAL.

[*Rising.*] Why, my dear good fellow——!

SOLNESS.

Yes, on my soul she does! I tell you it is so. And she has got you to think the same! Oh, I can assure you, doctor, I see it in your face as clearly as possible. You don't take me in so easily, I can tell you.

DR. HERDAL.

[*Looks at him in amazement.*] Never, Mr. Solness—never has such a thought entered my mind.

SOLNESS.

[*With an incredulous smile.*] Really? Has it not?

DR. HERDAL.

No, never! Nor your wife's mind either, I am convinced. I could almost swear to that.

SOLNESS.

Well, I wouldn't advise you to. For, in a certain sense, you see, perhaps—perhaps she is not so far wrong in thinking something of the kind.

DR. HERDAL.

Come now, I really must say——

SOLNESS.

[*Interrupting, with a sweep of his hand.*] Well, well, my dear doctor—don't let us discuss this any further. We had better agree to differ. [*Changes to a tone of quiet amusement.*] But look here now, doctor—h'm——

DR. HERDAL.

Well?

SOLNESS.

Since you don't believe that I am—ill—and crazy—and mad, and so forth——

DR. HERDAL.

What then?

SOLNESS.

Then I daresay you fancy that I am an extremely happy man.

DR. HERDAL.

Is that mere fancy?

SOLNESS.

[*Laughs.*] No, no—of course not! Heaven forbid! Only think—to be Solness the master builder! Halvard Solness! What could be more delightful?

DR. HERDAL.

Yes, I must say it seems to me you have had the luck on your side to an astounding degree.

SOLNESS.

[*Suppresses a gloomy smile.*] So I have. I can't complain on that score.

DR. HERDAL.

First of all that grim old robbers' castle was

burnt down for you. And that was certainly a great piece of luck.

SOLNESS.

[*Seriously.*] It was the home of Aline's family. Remember that.

DR. HERDAL.

Yes, it must have been a great grief to her.

SOLNESS.

She has not got over it to this day—not in al these twelve or thirteen years.

DR. HERDAL.

Ah, but what followed must have been the worst blow for her.

SOLNESS.

The one thing with the other.

DR. HERDAL.

But you—yourself—you rose upon the ruins. You began as a poor boy from a country village—and now you are at the head of your profession. Ah, yes, Mr. Solness, you have undoubtedly had the luck on your side.

SOLNESS.

[*Looking at him with embarrassment.*] Yes, but that is just what makes me so horribly afraid.

DR. HERDAL.

Afraid? Because you have the luck on your side!

SOLNESS.

It terrifies me—terrifies me every hour of the day. For sooner or later the luck must turn, you see.

DR. HERDAL.

Oh nonsense! What should make the luck turn?

SOLNESS.

[*With firm assurance.*] The younger generation.

DR. HERDAL.

Pooh! The younger generation! You are not laid on the shelf yet, I should hope. Oh no—your position here is probably firmer now than it has ever been.

SOLNESS.

The luck will turn. I know it—I feel the day approaching. Some one or other will take it into his head to say: Give me a chance! And then all the rest will come clamouring after him, and shake their fists at me and shout: Make room—make room—make room! Yes, just you see, doctor—presently the younger generation will come knocking at my door——

DR. HERDAL.

[*Laughing.*] Well, and what if they do?

SOLNESS.

What if they do? Then there's an end of Halvard Solness.

[*There is a knock at the door on the left.*

SOLNESS.

[*Starts.*] What's that? Did you not hear something?

DR. HERDAL.

Some one is knocking at the door.

SOLNESS.

[*Loudly.*] Come in.

HILDA WANGEL *enters by the hall door. She is of middle height, supple, and delicately built. Somewhat sunburnt. Dressed in a tourist costume, with skirt caught up for walking, a sailor's collar open at the throat, and a small sailor hat on her head. Knapsack on back, plaid in strap, and alpenstock.*

HILDA.

[*Goes straight up to* SOLNESS, *her eyes sparkling with happiness.*] Good evening!

SOLNESS.

[*Looks doubtfully at her.*] Good evening——

HILDA.

[*Laughs.*] I almost believe you don't recognise me!

SOLNESS.

No—I must admit that—just for the moment——

DR. HERDAL.

[*Approaching.*] But *I* recognise you, my dear young lady——

HILDA.

[*Pleased.*] Oh, is it you that——

DR. HERDAL.

Of course it is. [*To* SOLNESS.] We met at one of the mountain stations this summer. [*To* HILDA.] What became of the other ladies?

HILDA.

Oh, they went westward.

DR. HERDAL.

They didn't much like all the fun we used to have in the evenings.

HILDA.

No, I believe they didn't.

DR. HERDAL.

[*Holds up his finger at her.*] And I am afraid it can't be denied that you flirted a little with us.

HILDA.

Well, that was better fun than to sit there knitting stockings with all those old women.

DR. HERDAL.

[*Laughs.*] There I entirely agree with you!

SOLNESS.

Have you come to town this evening?

HILDA.

Yes, I have just arrived.

DR. HERDAL.

Quite alone, Miss Wangel?

HILDA.

Oh yes!

SOLNESS.

Wangel? Is your name Wangel?

HILDA.

[*Looks in amused surprise at him.*] Yes, of course it is.

SOLNESS.

Then you must be a daughter of the district doctor up at Lysanger?

HILDA.

[*As before.*] Yes, who else's daughter should I be?

SOLNESS.

Oh, then I suppose we met up there, that summer when I was building a tower on the old church.

HILDA.

[*More seriously.*] Yes, of course it was then we met.

SOLNESS.

Well, that is a long time ago.

HILDA.

[*Looks hard at him.*] It is exactly the ten years.

SOLNESS.

You must have been a mere child then, I should think.

HILDA.

[*Carelessly.*] Well, I was twelve or thirteen.

DR. HERDAL.

Is this the first time you have ever been up to town, Miss Wangel?

HILDA.

Yes, it is indeed.

SOLNESS.

And don't you know any one here

HILDA.

Nobody but you. And of course, your wife.

SOLNESS.

So you know her, too?

HILDA.

Only a little. We spent a few days together at the sanatorium.

SOLNESS.

Ah, up there?

HILDA.

She said I might come and pay her a visit if ever I came up to town. [*Smiles.*] Not that that was necessary.

SOLNESS.

Odd that she should never have mentioned it.

[HILDA *puts her stick down by the stove, takes off the knapsack and lays it and the plaid on the sofa.* DR. HERDAL *offers to help her.* SOLNESS *stands and gazes at her.*

HILDA.

[*Going towards him.*] Well, now I must ask you to let me stay the night here.

SOLNESS.

I am sure there will be no difficulty about that.

HILDA.

For I have no other clothes than those I stand in, except a change of linen in my knapsack. And that has to go to the wash, for it's very dirty.

SOLNESS.

Oh yes, that can be managed. Now I'll just let my wife know——

DR. HERDAL.

Meanwhile I will go and see my patient.

SOLNESS.

Yes, do; and come again later on.

DR. HERDAL.

[*Playfully, with a glance at* HILDA..] Oh that I will, you may be very certain! [*Laughs.*] So your prediction has come true, Mr. Solness!

SOLNESS.

How so?

DR. HERDAL.

The younger generation did come knocking at your door.

SOLNESS.

[*Cheerfully.*] Yes, but in a very different way fiom what I meant.

DR. HERDAL.

Very different, yes. That's undeniable.

[*He goes out by the hall-door.* SOLNESS *opens the door on the right and speaks into the side room.*

SOLNESS.

Aline! Will you come in here, please. Here is a friend of yours—Miss Wangel.

MRS. SOLNESS.

[*Appears in the doorway.*] Who do you say it is? [*Sees* HILDA.] Oh, is it you, Miss Wangel? [*Goes up to her and offers her hand.*] So you have come to town after all.

SOLNESS.

Miss Wangel has this moment arrived; and she would like to stay the night here.

MRS. SOLNESS.

Here with us? Oh yes, certainly.

SOLNESS.

Till she can get her things a little in order, you know.

MRS. SOLNESS.

I will do the best I can for you. It's no more than my duty. I suppose your trunk is coming on later?

HILDA.

I have no trunk.

MRS. SOLNESS.

Well, it will be all right, I daresay. In the meantime, you must excuse my leaving you here with my husband, until I can get a room made a little comfortable for you.

SOLNESS.

Can we not give her one of the nurseries? They are all ready as it is.

MRS. SOLNESS.

Oh yes. There we have room and to spare. [*To* HILDA.] Sit down now, and rest a little.

[*She goes out to the right.*

[HILDA, *with her hands behind her back, strolls about the room and looks at various objects.* SOLNESS *stands in front, beside the table, also with his hands behind his back, and follows her with his eyes.*

HILDA.

[*Stops and looks at him.*] Have you several nurseries?

SOLNESS.

There are three nurseries in the house.

HILDA.

That's a lot. Then I suppose you have a great many children?

SOLNESS.

No. We have no child. But now you can be the child here, for the time being.

HILDA.

For to-night, yes. I shall not cry. I mean to sleep as sound as a stone.

SOLNESS.

Yes, you must be very tired, I should think.

HILDA.

Oh no! But all the same—— It's so delicious to lie and dream.

SOLNESS.

Do you dream much of nights?

HILDA.

Oh yes! Almost always.

SOLNESS.

What do you dream about most?

HILDA.

I sha'n't tell you to-night. Another time—perhaps.

[*She again strolls about the room, stops at the desk and turns over the books and papers a little.*

SOLNESS.

[*Approaching.*] Are you searching for anything?

HILDA.

No, I am merely looking at all these things. [*Turns.*] Perhaps I mustn't?

SOLNESS.

Oh, by all means.

HILDA.

Is it you that write in this great ledger?

SOLNESS.

No, it's my book-keeper.

HILDA.

Is it a woman?

SOLNESS.

[*Smiles.*] Yes.

HILDA.

One you employ here, in your office?

SOLNESS.

Yes.

HILDA.

Is she married?

SOLNESS.

No, she is single.

HILDA.

Oh, indeed!

SOLNESS.

But I believe she is soon going to be married.

HILDA.

That's a good thing for her.

SOLNESS.

But not such a good thing for me. For then I shall have nobody to help me.

HILDA.

Can't you get hold of some one else who will do just as well?

SOLNESS.

Perhaps you would stay here and—and write in the ledger?

HILDA.

[*Measures him with a glance.*] Yes, I daresay! No, thank you—nothing of that sort for me.

[*She again strolls across the room, and sits down in the rocking-chair.* SOLNESS *too goes to the table.*

HILDA.

[*Continuing.*] For there must surely be plenty

of other things to be done here. [*Looks smilingly at him.*] Don't you think so, too?

SOLNESS.

Of course. First of all, I suppose, you want to make a round of the shops, and get yourself up in the height of fashion.

HILDA.

[*Amused.*] No, I think I shall let that alone!

SOLNESS.

Indeed?

HILDA.

For you must know I have run through all my money.

SOLNESS.

[*Laughs.*] Neither trunk nor money, then!

HILDA.

Neither one nor the other. But never mind—it doesn't matter now.

SOLNESS.

Come now, I like you for that.

HILDA.

Only for that?

SOLNESS.

For that among other things. [*Sits in the arm-chair.*] Is your father alive still?

HILDA.

Yes, father's alive.

SOLNESS.

Perhaps you are thinking of studying here?

HILDA.

No, that hadn't occurred to me.

SOLNESS.

But I suppose you will be staying for some time?

HILDA.

That must depend upon circumstances.

[*She sits awhile rocking herself and looking at him, half seriously, half with a suppressed smile. Then she takes off her hat and puts it on the table in front of her.*

HILDA.

Mr. Solness!

SOLNESS.

Well?

HILDA.

Have you a very bad memory?

SOLNESS.

A bad memory? No, not that I am aware of.

HILDA.

Then have you nothing to say to me about what happened up there?

SOLNESS.

[*In momentary surprise.*] Up at Lysanger? [*Indifferently.*] Why, it was nothing much to talk about, it seems to me.

HILDA.

[*Looks reproachfully at him.*] How can you sit there and say such things?

SOLNESS.

Well, then, you talk to me about it.

HILDA.

When the tower was finished, we had grand doings in the town.

SOLNESS.

Yes, I shall not easily forget that day.

HILDA.

[*Smiles.*] Will you not? That comes well from you.

SOLNESS.

Comes well?

HILDA.

There was music in the churchyard—and many, many hundreds of people. We school-girls were dressed in white; and we all carried flags.

SOLNESS.

Ah yes, those flags—I can tell you I remember them!

HILDA.

Then you climbed right up the scaffolding, straight to the very top; and you had a great wreath with you; and you hung that wreath right away up on the weather-vane.

SOLNESS.

[*Curtly interrupting.*] I always did that in those days. It is an old custom.

HILDA.

It was so wonderfully thrilling to stand below

and look up at you. Fancy, if he should fall over! He—the master builder himself!

SOLNESS.

[*As if to divert her from the subject.*] Yes, yes, yes, that might very well have happened, too. For one of those white-frocked little devils,—she went on in such a way, and screamed up at me so——

HILDA.

[*Sparkling with pleasure.*] "Hurra for Master Builder Solness!" Yes!

SOLNESS.

—and waved and flourished with her flag, so that I—so that it almost made me giddy to look at it.

HILDA.

[*In a lower voice, seriously.*] That little devil—that was *I*.

SOLNESS.

[*Fixes his eyes steadily upon her.*] I am sure of that now. It must have been you.

HILDA.

[*Lively again.*] Oh, it was so gloriously thrilling! I could not have believed there was a builder in the whole world that could build such a tremendously high tower. And then, that you yourself should stand at the very top of it, as large as life! And that you should not be the least bit dizzy! It was that above everything that made one—made one dizzy to think of.

SOLNESS.

How could you be so certain that I was not——?

HILDA.

[*Scouting the idea.*] No indeed! Oh no! I knew that instinctively. For if you had been, you could never have stood up there and sung.

SOLNESS.

[*Looks at her in astonishment*]. Sung? Did *I* sing?

HILDA.

Yes, I should think you did.

SOLNESS.

[*Shakes his head.*] I have never sung a note in my life.

HILDA.

Yes indeed, you sang then. It sounded like harps in the air.

SOLNESS.

[*Thoughtfully.*] This is very strange—all this.

HILDA.

[*Is silent awhile, looks at him and says in a low voice:*] But then,—it was after that—that the real thing happened.

SOLNESS.

The real thing?

HILDA.

[*Sparkling with vivacity.*] Yes, I surely don't need to remind you of that?

SOLNESS.

Oh yes, do remind me a little of that, too.

HILDA.

Don't you remember that a great dinner was given in your honour at the Club?

SOLNESS.

Yes, to be sure. It must have been the same afternoon, for I left the place next morning.

HILDA.

And from the Club you were invited to come round to our house to supper.

SOLNESS.

Quite right, Miss Wangel. It is wonderful how all these trifles have impressed themselves on your mind.

HILDA.

Trifles! I like that! Perhaps it was a trifle, too, that I was *alone* in the room when you came in?

SOLNESS.

Were you alone?

HILDA.

[*Without answering him.*] You didn't call me a little devil *then*?

SOLNESS.

No, I suppose I did not.

HILDA.

You said I was lovely in my white dress, and that I looked like a little princess.

SOLNESS.

I have no doubt you did, Miss Wangel.—And besides—I was feeling so buoyant and free that day——

HILDA.

And then you said that when I grew up I should be your princess.

SOLNESS.

[*Laughing a little.*] Dear, dear—did I say that too?

HILDA.

Yes, you did. And when I asked how long I should have to wait, you said that you would come again in ten years—like a troll—and carry me off—to Spain or some such place. And you promised you would buy me a kingdom there.

SOLNESS.

[*As before.*] Yes, after a good dinner one doesn't haggle about the halfpence. But did I really say all that

HILDA.

[*Laughs to herself.*] Yes. And you told me, too, what the kingdom was to be called.

SOLNESS.

Well, what was it?

HILDA.

It was to be called the kingdom of Orangia,[1] you said.

SOLNESS.

Well, that was an appetising name.

[1] In the original "Appelsinia," "appelsin" meaning "orange."

HILDA.

No, I didn't like it a bit; for it seemed as though you wanted to make game of me.

SOLNESS.

I am sure that cannot have been my intention.

HILDA.

No, I should hope not—considering what you did next——

SOLNESS.

What in the world did I do next?

HILDA.

Well, that's the finishing touch, if you have forgotten that too. I should have thought no one could help remembering such a thing as that.

SOLNESS.

Yes, yes, just give me a hint, and then perhaps—— Well?

HILDA.

[*Looks fixedly at him.*] You came and kissed me, Mr. Solness.

SOLNESS.

[*Open-mouthed, rising from his chair.*] *I* did!

HILDA.

Yes, indeed you did. You took me in both your arms, and bent my head back, and kissed me —many times.

SOLNESS.

Now really, my dear Miss Wangel——!

HILDA.

[*Rises.*] You surely cannot mean to deny it?

SOLNESS.

Yes, I do. I deny it altogether!

HILDA.

[*Looks scornfully at him.*] Oh, indeed!

[*She turns and goes slowly close up to the stove, where she remains standing motionless, her face averted from him, her hands behind her back. Short pause.*

SOLNESS.

[*Goes cautiously up behind her.*] Miss Wangel——!

HILDA.

[*Is silent and does not move.*]

SOLNESS.

Don't stand there like a statue. You must have dreamt all this. [*Lays his hand on her arm.*] Now just listen——

HILDA.

[*Makes an impatient movement with her arm.*]

SOLNESS.

[*As a thought flashes upon him.*] Or——! Wait a moment! There is something under all this, you may depend!

HILDA.

[*Does not move.*]

SOLNESS.

[*In a low voice, but with emphasis.*] I must have

thought all that. I must have wished it—have willed it—have longed to do it. And then——. May not that be the explanation?

HILDA.

[*Is still silent.*]

SOLNESS.

[*Impatiently.*] Oh very well, deuce take it all—then I did do it, I suppose.

HILDA.

[*Turns her head a little, but without looking at him.*] Then you admit it now?

SOLNESS.

Yes—whatever you like.

HILDA.

You came and put your arms round me?

SOLNESS.

Oh yes!

HILDA.

And bent my head back?

SOLNESS.

Very far back.

HILDA.

And kissed me?

SOLNESS.

Yes, I did

HILDA.

Many times?

SOLNESS.

As many as ever you like

HILDA.

[*Turns quickly towards him and has once more the sparkling expression of gladness in her eyes.*] Well, you see, I got it out of you at last!

SOLNESS.

[*With a slight smile.*] Yes--just think of my forgetting such a thing as that.

HILDA.

[*Again a little sulky, retreats from him.*] Oh, you have kissed so many people in your time, I suppose.

SOLNESS.

No, you mustn't think that of me. [HILDA *seats herself in the arm-chair.* SOLNESS *stands and leans against the rocking-chair. Looks observantly at her.*] Miss Wangel!

HILDA.

Yes!

SOLNESS.

How was it now? What came of all this—between us two?

HILDA.

Why, nothing more came of it. You know that quite well. For then the other guests came in, and then—bah!

SOLNESS.

Quite so! The others came in. To think of my forgetting that too!

HILDA.

Oh, you haven't really forgotten anything: you are only a little ashamed of it all. I am sure one doesn't forget things of that kind.

SOLNESS.

No, one would suppose not.

HILDA.

[*Lively again, looks at him.*] Perhaps you have even forgotten what day it was?

SOLNESS.

What day——?

HILDA.

Yes, on what day did you hang the wreath on the tower? Well? Tell me at once!

SOLNESS.

H'm—I confess I have forgotten the particular day. I only know it was ten years ago. Some time in the autumn.

HILDA.

[*Nods her head slowly several times.*] It was ten years ago—on the 19th of September.

SOLNESS.

Yes, it must have been about that time. Fancy your remembering that too! [*Stops.*] But wait a moment——! Yes—it's the 19th of September to-day.

HILDA.

Yes, it is; and the ten years are gone. And you didn't come—as you had promised me.

SOLNESS.

Promised you? Threatened, I suppose you mean?

HILDA.

I don't think there was any sort of threat in that.

SOLNESS.

Well then, a little bit of fun.

HILDA.

Was that all you wanted? To make fun of me?

SOLNESS.

Well, or to have a little joke with you. Upon my soul, I don't recollect. But it must have been something of that kind; for you were a mere child then.

HILDA.

Oh, perhaps I wasn't quite such a child either. Not such a mere chit as you imagine.

SOLNESS.

[*Looks searchingly at her.*] Did you really and seriously expect me to come again?

HILDA.

[*Conceals a half-teasing smile.*] Yes, indeed! I did expect that of you.

SOLNESS.

That I should come back to your home, and take you away with me?

HILDA.

Just like a troll—yes.

SOLNESS.

And make a princess of you?

HILDA.

That's what you promised.

SOLNESS.

And give you a kingdom as well?

HILDA.

[*Looks up at the ceiling.*] Why not? Of course it need not have been an actual, every-day sort of a kingdom.

SOLNESS.

But something else just as good?

HILDA.

Yes, at least as good. [*Looks at him a moment.*] I thought, if you could build the highest church-towers in the world, you could surely manage to raise a kingdom of one sort or another as well.

SOLNESS.

[*Shakes his head.*] I can't quite make you out, Miss Wangel.

HILDA.

Can you not? To me it seems all so simple.

SOLNESS.

No, I can't make up my mind whether you mean all you say, or are simply having a joke with me.

HILDA.

[*Smiles.*] Making fun of you, perhaps? I, too?

SOLNESS.

Yes, exactly. Making fun—of both of us. [*Looks at her.*] Is it long since you found out that I was married?

HILDA.

I have known it all along. Why do you ask me that?

SOLNESS.

[*Lightly.*] Oh, well, it just occurred to me. [*Looks earnestly at her, and says in a low voice.*] What have you come for?

HILDA.

I want my kingdom. The time is up.

SOLNESS.

[*Laughs involuntarily.*] What a girl you are!

HILDA.

[*Gaily.*] Out with my kingdom, Mr. Solness! [*Raps with her fingers.*] The kingdom on the table!

SOLNESS.

[*Pushing the rocking-chair nearer and sitting down.*] Now, seriously speaking—what have you come for? What do you really want to do here?

HILDA.

Oh, first of all, I want to go round and look at all the things that you have built.

SOLNESS.

That will give you plenty of exercise.

HILDA.

Yes, I know you have built a tremendous lot.

SOLNESS.

I have indeed—especially of late years.

HILDA

Many church-towers among the rest? Immensely high ones?

SOLNESS.

No. I build no more church-towers now. Nor churches either.

HILDA.

What *do* you build then?

SOLNESS.

Homes for human beings.

HILDA.

[*Reflectively.*] Couldn't you build a little—a little bit of a church-tower over these homes as well?

SOLNESS.

[*Starting.*] What do you mean by *that*?

HILDA.

I mean—something that points—points up into the free air. With the vane at a dizzy height.

SOLNESS.

[*Pondering a little.*] Strange that you should say *that*—for that is just what I am most anxious to do.

HILDA.

[*Impatiently.*] Why don't you do it, then?

SOLNESS.

[*Shakes his head.*] No, the people will not have it.

HILDA.

Fancy their not wanting it!

SOLNESS.

[*More lightly.*] But now I am building a new home for myself—just opposite here.

HILDA.

For yourself?

SOLNESS.

Yes. It is almost finished. And on that there is a tower.

HILDA.

A high tower?

SOLNESS.

Yes.

HILDA.

Very high?

SOLNESS.

No doubt people will say it is too high—too high for a dwelling-house.

HILDA.

I'll go out and look at that tower the first thing to-morrow morning.

SOLNESS.

[*Sits resting his cheek on his hand, and gazes at her.*] Tell me, Miss Wangel—what is your name? Your Christian name, I mean?

HILDA.

Why, Hilda, of course.

SOLNESS.

[*As before.*] Hilda? Indeed?

HILDA.

Don't you remember that? You called me Hilda yourself—that day when you misbehaved.

SOLNESS.

Did I really?

HILDA.

But then you said "little Hilda"; and I didn't like that.

SOLNESS.

Oh, you didn't like that, Miss Hilda?

HILDA.

No, not at such a time as that. But—"Princess Hilda"—that will sound very well, I think.

SOLNESS.

Very well indeed. Princess Hilda of—of—what was to be the name of the kingdom?

HILDA.

Pooh! I won't have anything to do with that stupid kingdom. I have set my heart upon quite a different one!

SOLNESS.

[*Has leaned back in the chair, still gazing at her.*] Isn't it strange——? The more I think of it now, the more it seems to me as though I had gone about all these years torturing myself with—h'm——

HILDA.

With what?

SOLNESS.

With the effort to recover something—some experience, which I seemed to have forgotten. But I never had the least inkling of what it could be.

HILDA.

You should have tied a knot in your pocket-handkerchief, Mr. Solness.

SOLNESS.

In that case, I should simply have had to go racking my brains to discover what the knot could mean.

HILDA.

Oh yes, I suppose there are trolls of that kind in the world, too.

SOLNESS.

[*Rises slowly.*] What a good thing it is that you have come to me now.

HILDA.

[*Looks deeply into his eyes.*] Is it a good thing!

SOLNESS.

For I have been so lonely here. I have been gazing so helplessly at it all. [*In a lower voice.*] I must tell you—I have begun to be so afraid—so terribly afraid of the younger generation.

HILDA.

[*With a little snort of contempt.*] Pooh—is the younger generation a thing to be afraid of?

SOLNESS.

It is indeed. And that is why I have locked and barred myself in. [*Mysteriously*] I tell you the younger generation will one day come and thunder at my door! They will break in upon me!

HILDA.

Then I should say you ought to go out and open the door to the younger generation.

SOLNESS.

Open the door?

HILDA.

Yes. Let them come in to you on friendly terms, as it were.

SOLNESS.

No, no, no! The younger generation—it means retribution, you see. It comes, as if under a new banner, heralding the turn of fortune.

HILDA.

[*Rises, looks at him, and says with a quivering twitch of her lips.*] Can *I* be of any use to you, Mr. Solness?

SOLNESS.

Yes, you can indeed! For you, too, come—under a new banner, it seems to me. Youth marshalled against youth——!

DR. HERDAL *comes in by the hall-door.*

DR. HERDAL.

What—you and Miss Wangel here still?

SOLNESS.

Yes. We have had no end of things to talk about.

HILDA.

Both old and new.

DR. HERDAL.

Have you really?

HILDA.

Oh, it has been the greatest fun. For Mr. Solness—he has such a miraculous memory. All the least little details he remembers instantly.

MRS. SOLNESS *enters by the door on the right.*

MRS. SOLNESS.

Well, Miss Wangel, your room is quite ready for you now.

HILDA.

Oh, how kind you are to me!

SOLNESS.

[*To* MRS. SOLNESS.] The nursery?

MRS. SOLNESS.

Yes, the middle one. But first let us go in to supper.

SOLNESS.

[*Nods to* HILDA.] Hilda shall sleep in the nursery, she shall.

MRS. SOLNESS.

[*Looks at him.*] Hilda?

SOLNESS.

Yes, Miss Wangel's name is Hilda. I knew her when she was a child.

MRS. SOLNESS.

Did you really, Halvard? Well, shall we go? Supper is on the table.

[*She takes* DR. HERDAL'S *arm and goes out with him to the right.* HILDA *has meanwhile been collecting her travelling things.*

HILDA.

[*Softly and rapidly to* SOLNESS.] Is it true, what you said? Can I be of use to you?

SOLNESS.

[*Takes the things from her.*] You are the very being I have needed most.

HILDA.

[*Looks at him with happy, wondering eyes and clasps her hands.*] But then, great heavens——!

SOLNESS.

[*Eagerly.*] What——?

HILDA.

Then I have my kingdom!

SOLNESS.

[*Involuntarily.*] Hilda——!

HILDA.

[*Again with the quivering twitch of her lips.*] Almost—I was going to say.

[*She goes out to the right,* SOLNESS *follows her.*

ACT SECOND.

A prettily furnished small drawing-room in SOLNESS'S *house. In the back, a glass-door leading out to the verandah and garden. The right-hand corner is cut off transversely by a large bay-window, in which are flower-stands. The left-hand corner is similarly cut off by a transverse wall, in which is a small door papered like the wall. On each side, an ordinary door. In front, on the right, a console table with a large mirror over it. Well-filled stands of plants and flowers. In front, on the left, a sofa with a table and chairs. Further back, a bookcase. Well forward in the room, before the bay window, a small table and some chairs. It is early in the day.*

SOLNESS *sits by the little table with* RAGNAR BROVIK'S *portfolio open in front of him. He is turning the drawings over and closely examining some of them.* MRS. SOLNESS *moves about noiselessly with a small watering-pot, attending to her flowers. She is dressed in black as before. Her hat, cloak and parasol lie on a chair near the mirror. Unobserved by her,* SOLNESS *now and again follows her with his eyes. Neither of them speaks.*

KAIA FOSLI *enters quietly by the door on the left.*

SOLNESS.

[*Turns his head, and says in an off-hand tone of indifference*] Well, is that you?

KAIA.

I merely wished to let you know that I have come.

SOLNESS.

Yes, yes, that's all right. Hasn't Ragnar come too?

KAIA.

No, not yet. He had to wait a little while to see the doctor. But he is coming presently to hear——

SOLNESS.

How is the old man to-day?

KAIA.

Not well. He begs you to excuse him; he is obliged to keep his bed to-day.

SOLNESS.

Why, of course; by all means let him rest. But now, get to your work.

KAIA.

Yes. [*Pauses at the door.*] Do you wish to speak to Ragnar when he comes?

SOLNESS.

No—I don't know that I have anything particular to say to him.

[KAIA *goes out again to the left.* SOLNESS *remains seated, turning over the drawings.*

MRS. SOLNESS.

[*Over beside the plants.*] I wonder if he isn't going to die now, as well?

SOLNESS.

[*Looks up at her.*] As well as who?

MRS. SOLNESS.

[*Without answering.*] Yes, yes—depend upon it, Halvard, old Brovik is going to die too. You'll see that he will.

SOLNESS.

My dear Aline, ought you not to go out for a little walk?

MRS. SOLNESS.

Yes, I suppose I ought to.

[*She continues to attend to the flowers.*

SOLNESS.

[*Bending over the drawings.*] Is she still asleep?

MRS. SOLNESS.

[*Looking at him.*] Is it Miss Wangel you are sitting there thinking about?

SOLNESS.

[*Indifferently.*] I just happened to recollect her.

MRS. SOLNESS.

Miss Wangel was up long ago.

SOLNESS.

Oh, was she?

MRS. SOLNESS.

When I went in to see her, she was busy putting her things in order.

[*She goes in front of the mirror and slowly begins to put on her hat.*

SOLNESS.

[*After a short pause.*] So we have found a use for one of our nurseries after all, Aline.

MRS. SOLNESS.

Yes, we have.

SOLNESS.

That seems to me better than to have them all standing empty.

MRS. SOLNESS.

That emptiness is dreadful; you are right there.

SOLNESS.

[*Closes the portfolio, rises and approaches her.*] You will find that we shall get on far better after this, Aline. Things will be more comfortable. Life will be easier—especially for you.

MRS. SOLNESS.

[*Looks at him.*] After this?

SOLNESS.

Yes, believe me, Aline——

MRS. SOLNESS.

Do you mean—because she has come here?

SOLNESS.

[*Checking himself.*] I mean, of course—when once we have moved into the new house.

MRS. SOLNESS.

[*Takes her cloak.*] Ah, do you think so, Halvard? Will it be better then?

SOLNESS.

I can't think otherwise. And surely you think so too?

MRS. SOLNESS.

I think nothing at all about the new house.

SOLNESS.

[*Cast down.*] It's hard for me to hear you say that; for you know it is mainly for your sake that I have built it.

[*He offers to help her on with her cloak.*

MRS. SOLNESS.

[*Evades him.*] The fact is, you do far too much for my sake.

SOLNESS.

[*With a certain vehemence.*] No, no, you really mustn't say that, Aline! I cannot bear to hear you say such things!

MRS. SOLNESS.

Very well, then I won't say it, Halvard.

SOLNESS.

But I stick to what *I* said. You'll see that things will be easier for you in the new place.

MRS. SOLNESS.

Oh heavens—easier for me——!

SOLNESS.

[*Eagerly.*] Yes, indeed they will! You may be quite sure of that! For you see—there will be so very, very much there that will remind you of your own home——

MRS. SOLNESS.

The home that used to be father's and mother's —and that was burnt to the ground——

SOLNESS.

[*In a low voice.*] Yes, yes, my poor Aline. That was a terrible blow for you.

MRS. SOLNESS.

[*Breaking out in lamentation.*] You may build as much as ever you like, Halvard—you can never build up again a real home for me!

SOLNESS.

[*Crosses the room.*] Well, in Heaven's name, let us talk no more about it then.

MRS. SOLNESS.

We are not in the habit of talking about it. For you always put the thought away from you——

SOLNESS.

[*Stops suddenly and looks at her.*] Do I? And why should I do that? Put the thought away from me?

MRS. SOLNESS.

Oh yes, Halvard, I understand you very well. You are so anxious to spare me—and to find excuses for me too—as much as ever you can.

SOLNESS.

[*With astonishment in his eyes.*] You! Is it you —yourself, that you are talking about, Aline?

MRS. SOLNESS.

Yes, who else should it be but myself?

SOLNESS.

[*Involuntarily to himself.*] That too!

MRS. SOLNESS.

As for the old house, I wouldn't mind so much about that. When once misfortune was in the air —why——

SOLNESS.

Ah, you are right there. Misfortune will have its way—as the saying goes.

MRS. SOLNESS.

But it's what came of the fire—the dreadful thing that followed——! That is the thing! That, that, that!

SOLNESS.

[*Vehemently.*] Don't think about that, Aline!

MRS. SOLNESS.

Ah, that is exactly what I cannot help thinking about. And now, at last, I must speak about it, too; for I don't seem able to bear it any longer. And then never to be able to forgive myself——

SOLNESS.

[*Exclaiming.*] Yourself——!

MRS. SOLNESS.

Yes, for I had duties on both sides—both towards you and towards the little ones. I ought to have hardened myself—not to have let the horror take such hold upon me—nor the grief for the burning of my home. [*Wrings her hands.*] Oh, Halvard, if I had only had the strength!

SOLNESS.

[*Softly, much moved, comes closer.*] Aline—you must promise me never to think these thoughts any more.—Promise me that, dear!

MRS. SOLNESS.

Oh, promise, promise! One can promise anything.

SOLNESS.

[*Clenches his hands and crosses the room.*] Oh, but this is hopeless, hopeless! Never a ray of sunlight! Not so much as a gleam of brightness to light up our home!

MRS. SOLNESS.

This is no home, Halvard.

SOLNESS.

Oh no, you may well say that. [*Gloomily.*] And God knows whether you are not right in saying that it will be no better for us in the new house, either.

MRS. SOLNESS.

It will never be any better. Just as empty—just as desolate—there as here.

SOLNESS.

[*Vehemently.*] Why in all the world have we built it then? Can you tell me that?

MRS. SOLNESS.

No; you must answer that question for yourself.

SOLNESS.

[*Glances suspiciously at her.*] What do you mean by that, Aline?

MRS. SOLNESS.

What do I mean?

SOLNESS.

Yes, in the devil's name! You said it so strangely—as if you had some hidden meaning in it.

MRS. SOLNESS.

No, indeed, I assure you——

SOLNESS.

[*Comes closer.*] Oh, come now—I know what I know. I have both my eyes and my ears about me, Aline—you may depend upon that!

MRS. SOLNESS.

Why, what are you talking about? What is it?

SOLNESS.

[*Places himself in front of her.*] Do you mean to say you don't find a kind of lurking, hidden meaning in the most innocent word I happen to say?

MRS. SOLNESS.

I, do you say? *I* do that?

SOLNESS.

[*Laughs.*] Ho-ho-ho! It's natural enough, Aline! When you have a sick man on your hands——

MRS. SOLNESS.

[*Anxiously.*] Sick? Are you ill, Halvard?

SOLNESS.

[*Violently.*] A half-mad man then! A crazy man! Call me what you will.

MRS. SOLNESS.

[*Feels blindly for a chair and sits down.*] Halvard—for God's sake——

SOLNESS.

But you are wrong, both you and the doctor. I am not in the state you imagine.

[*He walks up and down the room.* MRS. SOLNESS *follows him anxiously with her eyes. Finally he goes up to her.*

SOLNESS.

[*Calmly.*] In reality there is nothing whatever the matter with me.

MRS. SOLNESS.

No, there isn't, is there? But then what is it that troubles you so?

SOLNESS.

Why this, that I often feel ready to sink under this terrible burden of debt——

MRS. SOLNESS.

Debt, do you say? But you owe no one anything, Halvard!

SOLNESS.

[*Softly, with emotion.*] I owe a boundless debt to you—to you—to you, Aline.

MRS. SOLNESS.

[*Rises slowly.*] What is behind all this? You may just as well tell me at once.

SOLNESS.

But there is nothing behind it! I have never done you any wrong—not wittingly and wilfully, at any rate And yet—and yet it seems as though a crushing debt rested upon me and weighed me down.

MRS. SOLNESS.

A debt to me?

SOLNESS.

Chiefly to you.

MRS. SOLNESS.

Then you are—ill after all, Halvard.

SOLNESS.

[*Gloomily.*] I suppose I must be—or not far from it. [*Looks towards the door to the right, which is opened at this moment.*] Ah! now it grows lighter.

HILDA WANGEL *comes in. She has made some alteration in her dress, and let down her skirt.*

HILDA.

Good morning, Mr. Solness!

SOLNESS.

[*Nods.*] Slept well?

HILDA.

Quite deliciously! Like a child in a cradle. Oh—I lay and stretched myself like—like a princess!

SOLNESS.

[*Smiles a little.*] You were thoroughly comfortable then?

HILDA.

I should think so.

SOLNESS.

And no doubt you dreamed, too.

HILDA.

Yes, I did. But that was horrid.

SOLNESS.

Was it?

HILDA.

Yes, for I dreamed I was falling over a frightfully high, sheer precipice. Do you never have that kind of dream?

SOLNESS.

Oh yes—now and then——

HILDA.

It's tremendously thrilling—when you fall and fall——

SOLNESS.

It seems to make one's blood run cold.

HILDA.

Do you draw your legs up under you while you are falling?

SOLNESS.

Yes, as high as ever I can.

HILDA.

So do I.

MRS. SOLNESS.

[*Takes her parasol.*] I must go into town now, Halvard. [*To* HILDA.] And I'll try to get one or two things that you may require.

HILDA.

[*Making a motion to throw her arms round her neck.*] Oh, you dear, sweet Mrs. Solness! You are really much too kind to me! Frightfully kind——

MRS. SOLNESS.

[*Deprecatingly, freeing herself.*] Oh, not at all. It's only my duty, so I am very glad to do it.

HILDA.

[*Offended, pouts.*] But really, I think I am quite fit to be seen in the streets—now that I've put my dress to rights. Or do you think I am not?

MRS. SOLNESS.

To tell you the truth, I think people would stare at you a little.

HILDA.

[*Contemptuously.*] Pooh! Is that all? That only amuses me.

SOLNESS.

[*With suppressed ill-humour.*] Yes, but people might take it into their heads that you were mad too, you see.

HILDA.

Mad? Are there so many mad people here in town, then?

SOLNESS.

[*Points to his own forehead.*] Here you see one at all events.

HILDA.

You—Mr. Solness!

MRS. SOLNESS.

Oh, don't talk like that, my dear Halvard!

SOLNESS.

Have you not noticed that yet?

HILDA.

No, I certainly have not. [*Reflects and laughs a little.*] And yet—perhaps in one single thing.

SOLNESS.

Ah, do you hear that, Aline?

MRS SOLNESS.

What is that one single thing, Miss Wangel?

HILDA.

No, I won't say.

SOLNESS.

Oh yes, do!

HILDA.

No thank you—I am not so mad as that.

MRS. SOLNESS.

When you and Miss Wangel are alone, I daresay she will tell you, Halvard.

SOLNESS.

Ah—you think she will?

MRS. SOLNESS.

Oh yes, certainly. For you have known her so well in the past. Ever since she was a child—you tell me. [*She goes out by the door on the left.*

HILDA.

[*After a little while.*] Does your wife dislike me very much?

SOLNESS.

Did you think you noticed anything of the kind?

HILDA.

Did you not notice it yourself?

SOLNESS.

[*Evasively.*] Aline has become exceedingly shy with strangers of late years.

HILDA.

Has she really?

SOLNESS.

But if only you could get to know her thoroughly——! Ah, she is so good—so kind—so excellent a creature——

HILDA.

[*Impatiently.*] But if she is all that—what made her say that about her duty?

SOLNESS.

Her duty?

HILDA.

She said that she would go out and buy something for me, because it was her duty. Oh I can't bear that ugly, horrid word!

SOLNESS.

Why not?

HILDA.

It sounds so cold, and sharp, and stinging. Duty—duty—duty. Don't you think so, too? Doesn't it seem to sting you?

SOLNESS.

H'm—haven't thought much about it.

HILDA.

Yes, it does. And if she is so good—as you say she is—why should she talk in that way?

SOLNESS.

But, good Lord, what would you have had her say, then?

HILDA.

She might have said she would do it because she had taken a tremendous fancy to me. She might have said something like that—something really warm and cordial, you understand.

SOLNESS.

[*Looks at her.*] Is that how you would like to have it?

HILDA.

Yes, precisely. [*She wanders about the room, stops at the bookcase and looks at the books.*] What a lot of books you have.

SOLNESS.

Yes, I have got together a good many.

HILDA.

Do you read them all, too?

SOLNESS.

I used to try to. Do you read much?

HILDA.

No, never! I have given it up. For it all seems so irrelevant.

SOLNESS.

That is just my feeling.

[HILDA *wanders about a little, stops at the small table, opens the portfolio and turns over the contents.*

HILDA.

Are all these drawings yours?

SOLNESS.

No, they are drawn by a young man whom I employ to help me.

HILDA.

Some one you have taught?

SOLNESS.

Oh yes, no doubt he has learnt something from me, too.

HILDA.

[*Sits down.*] Then I suppose he is very clever. [*Looks at a drawing.*] Isn't he?

SOLNESS.

Oh, he might be worse. For my purpose——

HILDA.

Oh yes—I'm sure he is frightfully clever.

SOLNESS.

Do you think you can see that in the drawings?

HILDA.

Pooh—these scrawlings! But if he has been learning from you——

SOLNESS.

Oh, so far as that goes——there are plenty of people here that have learnt from me, and have come to little enough for all that.

HILDA.

[*Looks at him and shakes her head.*] No, I can't for the life of me understand how you can be so stupid.

SOLNESS.

Stupid? Do you think I am so very stupid?

HILDA.

Yes, I do indeed If you are content to go about here teaching all these people——

SOLNESS.

[*With a slight start.*] Well, and why not?

HILDA.

[*Rises, half serious, half laughing.*] No indeed, Mr. Solness! What can be the good of that? No one but you should be allowed to build. You should stand quite alone—do it all yourself. Now you know it.

SOLNESS.

[*Involuntarily.*] Hilda——!

HILDA.

Well!

SOLNESS.

How in the world did that come into your head?

HILDA.

Do you think I am so very far wrong then?

SOLNESS.

No, that's not what I mean. But now I'll tell you something.

HILDA.

Well?

SOLNESS.

I keep on—incessantly—in silence and alone—brooding on that very thought.

HILDA.

Yes, that seems to me perfectly natural.

SOLNESS.

[*Looks somewhat searchingly at her.*] Perhaps you have noticed it already?

HILDA.

No, indeed I haven't.

SOLNESS.

But just now—when you said you thought I was—off my balance? In one thing, you said——

HILDA.

Oh, I was thinking of something quite different.

SOLNESS.

What was it

HILDA.

I am not going to tell you.

SOLNESS.

[*Crosses the room.*] Well, well—as you please. [*Stops at the bow-window.*] Come here, and I will show you something.

HILDA.

[*Approaching.*] What is it?

SOLNESS.

Do you see—over there in the garden——?

HILDA.

Yes?

SOLNESS.

[*Points.*] Right above the great quarry——?

HILDA.

That new house, you mean?

SOLNESS.

The one that is being built, yes. Almost finished.

HILDA.

It seems to have a very high tower.

SOLNESS.

The scaffolding is still up.

HILDA.

Is that your new house?

SOLNESS.

Yes.

HILDA.

The house you are soon going to move into?

SOLNESS.

Yes.

HILDA.

[*Looks at him.*] Are there nurseries in that house, too?

SOLNESS.

Three, as there are here.

HILDA.

And no child.

SOLNESS.

And there never will be one.

HILDA.

[*With a half-smile.*] Well, isn't it just as I said——?

SOLNESS.

That——?

HILDA.

That you are a little—a little mad after all.

SOLNESS.

Was that what you were thinking of?

HILDA.

Yes, of all the empty nurseries I slept in.

SOLNESS.

[*Lowers his voice.*] We have had children—Aline and I.

HILDA.

[*Looks eagerly at him.*] Have you——?

SOLNESS.

Two little boys. They were of the same age.

HILDA.

Twins, then.

SOLNESS.

Yes, twins. It's eleven or twelve years ago now.

HILDA.

[*Cautiously.*] And so both of them——? You have lost both the twins, then?

SOLNESS.

[*With quiet emotion.*] We kept them only about three weeks. Or scarcely so much. [*Bursts forth.*] Oh, Hilda, I can't tell you what a good thing it is for me that you have come! For now at last I have some one I can talk to!

HILDA.

Can you not talk to—*her*, too?

SOLNESS.

Not about this. Not as I want to talk and must talk. [*Gloomily.*] And not about so many other things, either.

HILDA.

[*In a subdued voice.*] Was that all you meant when you said you needed me?

SOLNESS.

That was mainly what I meant—at all events, yesterday. For to-day I am not so sure—[*Breaking off.*] Come here and let us sit down, Hilda. Sit there on the sofa—so that you can look into the garden. [HILDA *seats herself in the corner of the sofa.* SOLNESS *brings a chair closer.*] Should you like to hear about it?

HILDA.

Yes, I shall love to sit and listen to you.

SOLNESS.

[*Sits down.*] Then I will tell you all about it.

HILDA.

Now I can see both the garden and you, Mr. Solness. So now, tell away! Begin!

SOLNESS.

[*Points towards the bow-window.*] Out there on the rising ground—where you see the new house——

HILDA.

Yes?

SOLNESS.

Aline and I lived there in the first years of our married life. There was an old house up there that had belonged to her mother; and we inherited it, and the whole of the great garden with it.

HILDA.

Was there a tower on that house, too?

SOLNESS.

No, nothing of the kind. From the outside it looked like a great, dark, ugly wooden box; but all the same, it was snug and comfortable enough inside.

HILDA.

Then did you pull down the ramshackle old place?

SOLNESS.

No, it was burnt down.

HILDA.

The whole of it?

SOLNESS.

Yes.

HILDA.

Was that a great misfortune for you?

SOLNESS.

That depends on how you look at it. As a builder, the fire was the making of me——

HILDA.

Well, but——?

SOLNESS.

It was just after the birth of the two little boys——

HILDA.

The poor little twins, yes.

SOLNESS.

They came healthy and bonny into the world.

And they were growing too—you could see the difference from day to day.

HILDA.

Little children do grow quickly at first.

SOLNESS.

It was the prettiest sight in the world to see Aline lying with the two of them in her arms. —But then came the night of the fire——

HILDA.

[*Excitedly.*] What happened? Do tell me! Was any one burnt?

SOLNESS.

No, not that. Every one got safe and sound out of the house——

HILDA.

Well, and what then——?

SOLNESS.

The fright had shaken Aline terribly. The alarm—the escape—the break-neck hurry—and then the ice-cold night air—for they had to be carried out just as they lay—both she and the little ones.

HILDA.

Was it too much for them?

SOLNESS.

Oh no, they stood it well enough. But Aline fell into a fever, and it affected her milk. She would insist on nursing them herself; because it was her duty, she said. And both our little boys, they—[*Clenching his hands.*]—they—oh !

HILDA.

They did not get over *that*?

SOLNESS.

No, *that* they did not get over. *That* was how we lost them.

HILDA.

It must have been terribly hard for you.

SOLNESS.

Hard enough for me; but ten times harder for Aline. [*Clenching his hands in suppressed fury*.] Oh, that such things should be allowed to happen here in the world! [*Shortly and firmly.*] From the day I lost them, I had no heart for building churches.

HILDA.

Did you not like building the church-tower in our town?

SOLNESS.

I didn't like it. I know how free and happy I felt when that tower was finished.

HILDA.

I know that, too.

SOLNESS.

And now I shall never—never build anything of that sort again! Neither churches nor church-towers.

HILDA.

[*Nods slowly.*] Nothing but houses for people to live in.

SOLNESS.

Homes for human beings, Hilda.

HILDA.

But homes with high towers and pinnacles upon them.

SOLNESS.

If possible. [*Adopts a lighter tone.*] But, as I said before, that fire was the making of me—as a builder, I mean.

HILDA.

Why don't you call yourself an architect, like the others?

SOLNESS.

I have not been systematically enough taught for that. Most of what I know I have found out for myself.

HILDA.

But you succeeded all the same.

SOLNESS.

Yes, thanks to the fire. I laid out almost the whole of the garden in villa lots; and *there* I was able to build after my own heart. So I came to the front with a rush.

HILDA.

[*Looks keenly at him.*] You must surely be a very happy man, as matters stand with you.

SOLNESS.

[*Gloomily.*] Happy? Do *you* say that, too—like all the rest of them?

HILDA.

Yes, I should say you must be. If you could only cease thinking about the two little children——

SOLNESS.

[*Slowly.*] The two little children—they are not so easy to forget, Hilda.

HILDA.

[*Somewhat uncertainly.*] Do you still feel their loss so much—after all these years?

SOLNESS.

[*Looks fixedly at her, without replying.*] A happy man you said——

HILDA.

Well, now, are you not happy—in other respects?

SOLNESS.

[*Continues to look at her.*] When I told you all this about the fire—h'm——

HILDA.

Well?

SOLNESS.

Was there not one special thought that you—that you seized upon?

HILDA.

[*Reflects in vain.*] No. What thought should that be?

SOLNESS.

[*With subdued emphasis.*] It was simply and solely by that fire that I was enabled to build homes for human beings. Cosy, comfortable, bright homes, where father and mother and the whole troop of children can live in safety and gladness, feeling what a happy thing it is to be alive in the world—and most of all to belong to each other—in great things and in small.

HILDA.

[*Ardently.*] Well, and is it not a great happiness for you to be able to build such beautiful homes?

SOLNESS.

The price, Hilda! The terrible price I had to pay for the opportunity!

HILDA.

But can you never get over that?

SOLNESS.

No. That I might build homes for others, I had to forego—to forego for all time—the home that might have been my own. I mean a home for a troop of children—and for father and mother, too.

HILDA.

[*Cautiously.*] But need you have done that? For all time, you say?

SOLNESS.

[*Nods slowly.*] That was the price of this happiness that people talk about. [*Breathes heavily.*] This happiness—h'm—this happiness was not to be bought any cheaper, Hilda.

HILDA.

[*As before.*] But may it not come right even yet?

SOLNESS.

Never in this world—never. That is another consequence of the fire—and of Aline's illness afterwards.

HILDA.

[*Looks at him with an indefinable expression.*] And yet you build all these nurseries?

SOLNESS.

[*Seriously.*] Have you never noticed, Hilda, how the impossible—how it seems to beckon and cry aloud to one?

HILDA.

[*Reflecting.*] The impossible? [*With animation.*] Yes, indeed! Is that how you feel too?

SOLNESS.

Yes, I do.

HILDA.

Then there must be—a little of the troll in you too.

SOLNESS.

Why of the troll?

HILDA.

What would you call it, then?

SOLNESS.

[*Rises.*] Well, well, perhaps you are right. [*Vehemently.*] But how can I help turning into a troll, when this is how it always goes with me in everything—in everything!

HILDA.

How do you mean?

SOLNESS.

[*Speaking low, with inward emotion.*] Mark what I say to you, Hilda. All that I have succeeded in doing, building, creating—all the beauty, security, cheerful comfort—ay, and magnificence too—[*Clenches his hands.*] Oh, is it not terrible even to think of——!

HILDA.

What is so terrible?

SOLNESS.

That all this I have to make up for, to pay for—not in money, but in human happiness. And not with my own happiness only, but with other people's too. Yes, yes, do you see *that*, Hilda? That is the price which my position as an artist has cost me—and others And every single day I have to look on while the price is paid for me anew. Over again, and over again—and over again for ever!

HILDA.

[*Rises and looks steadily at him.*] Now I can see that you are thinking of—of *her*.

SOLNESS.

Yes, mainly of Aline. For Aline—*she*, too, had her vocation in life, just as much as I had mine. [*His voice quivers.*] But her vocation has had to be stunted, and crushed, and shattered—in order that mine might force its way to—to a sort of great victory. For you must know that Aline—she, too, had a talent for building.

HILDA.

She! For building?

SOLNESS.

[*Shakes his head.*] Not houses and towers, and spires—not such things as I work away at——

HILDA.

Well, but what then?

SOLNESS.

[*Softly, with emotion.*] For building up the souls of little children, Hilda. For building up children's souls in perfect balance, and in noble and beautiful forms. For enabling them to soar up into erect and full-grown human souls. That was Aline's talent. And there it all lies now—unused and unusable for ever—of no earthly service to any one—just like the ruins left by a fire.

HILDA.

Yes, but even if this were so——?

SOLNESS.

It is so! It is so! I know it!

HILDA.

Well, but in any case it is not your fault.

SOLNESS.

[*Fixes his eyes on her, and nods slowly.*] Ah, that is the great, the terrible question. That is the doubt that is gnawing me—night and day.

HILDA.

That?

SOLNESS.

Yes. Suppose the fault was mine—in a certain sense.

HILDA.

Your fault! The fire!

SOLNESS.

All of it; the whole thing. And yet, perhaps—I may not have had anything to do with it.

HILDA.

[*Looks at him with a troubled expression*] Oh, Mr. Solness—if you can talk like that, I am afraid you must be—ill, after all.

SOLNESS.

H'm—I don't think I shall ever be of quite sound mind on that point.

RAGNAR BROVIK *cautiously opens the little door in the left-hand corner.* HILDA *comes forward.*

RAGNAR.

[*When he sees* HILDA.] Oh. I beg pardon, Mr. Solness—— [*He makes a movement to withdraw.*

SOLNESS.

No, no, don't go. Let us get it over.

RAGNAR.

Oh, yes—if only we could.

SOLNESS.

I hear your father is no better?

RAGNAR.

Father is fast growing weaker—and therefore I beg and implore you to write a few kind words for me on one of the plans! Something for father to read before he——

SOLNESS.

[*Vehemently.*] I won't hear anything more about those drawings of yours!

RAGNAR.

Have you looked at them?

SOLNESS.

Yes—I have.

RAGNAR.

And they are good for nothing? And *I* am good for nothing, too?

SOLNESS.

[*Evasively.*] Stay here with me, Ragnar. You shall have everything your own way. And then you can marry Kaia, and live at your ease—and happily too, who knows? Only don't think of building on your own account.

RAGNAR.

Well, well, then I must go home and tell father what you say—I promised I would.—Is this what I am to tell father—before he dies?

SOLNESS.

[*With a groan.*] Oh tell him—tell him what you will, for me. Best to say nothing at all to him! [*With a sudden outburst.*] I cannot do anything else, Ragnar!

RAGNAR.

May I have the drawings to take with me?

SOLNESS.

Yes, take them—take them by all means! They are lying there on the table.

RAGNAR.

[*Goes to the table.*] Thanks.

HILDA.

[*Puts her hand on the portfolio.*] No, no; leave them here.

SOLNESS.

Why?

HILDA.

Because I want to look at them, too.

SOLNESS

But you have been—— [*To* RAGNAR.] Well, leave them here, then.

RAGNAR.

Very well.

SOLNESS.

And go home at once to your father.

RAGNAR.

Yes, I suppose I must.

SOLNESS.

[*As if in desperation.*] Ragnar—you must not ask me to do what is beyond my power! Do you hear, Ragnar? You must not!

RAGNAR.

No, no. I beg your pardon——

[*He bows, and goes out by the corner door.* HILDA *goes over and sits down on a chair near the mirror.*

HILDA.

[*Looks angrily at* SOLNESS.] That was a very ugly thing to do.

SOLNESS.

Do you think so, too?

HILDA.

Yes, it was horribly ugly—and hard and bad and cruel as well.

SOLNESS.

Oh, you don't understand my position.

HILDA.

No matter——. I say you ought not to be like that.

SOLNESS.

You said yourself, only just now, that no one but *I* ought to be allowed to build.

HILDA.

I may say such things—but *you* must not.

SOLNESS.

I most of all, surely, who have paid so dear for my position.

HILDA.

Oh yes—with what you call domestic comfort —and that sort of thing.

SOLNESS.

And with my peace of soul into the bargain.

HILDA.

[*Rising.*] Peace of soul! [*With feeling.*] Yes, yes, you are right in that! Poor Mr. Solness—you fancy that——

SOLNESS.

[*With a quiet, chuckling laugh.*] Just sit down again, Hilda, and I'll tell you something funny.

HILDA.

[*Sits down; with intent interest.*] Well?

SOLNESS.

It sounds such a ludicrous little thing; for, you see, the whole story turns upon nothing but a crack in a chimney.

HILDA.

No more than that?

SOLNESS.

No, not to begin with.

[*He moves a chair nearer to* HILDA *and sits down.*

HILDA.

[*Impatiently, taps on her knee.*] Well, now for the crack in the chimney!

SOLNESS.

I had noticed the split in the flue long, long before the fire. Every time I went up into the attic, I looked to see if it was still there.

HILDA.

And it was?

SOLNESS.

Yes; for no one else knew about it.

HILDA.

And you said nothing?

SOLNESS.

Nothing.

HILDA.

And did not think of repairing the flue either?

SOLNESS.

Oh yes, I thought about it—but never got any further. Every time I intended to set to work, it seemed just as if a hand held me back. Not to-day, I thought—to-morrow; and nothing ever came of it.

HILDA.

But why did you keep putting it off like that?

SOLNESS.

Because I was revolving something in my mind. [*Slowly, and in a low voice.*] Through that little black crack in the chimney, I might, perhaps, force my way upwards—as a builder.

HILDA.

[*Looking straight in front of her.*] That must have been thrilling.

SOLNESS.

Almost irresistible—quite irresistible. For at that time it appeared to me a perfectly simple and straightforward matter. I would have had it happen in the winter-time—a little before midday. I was to be out driving Aline in the sleigh. The servants at home would have made huge fires in the stoves.

HILDA

For, of course, it was to be bitterly cold that day?

SOLNESS.

Rather biting, yes—and they would want Aline to find it thoroughly snug and warm when she came home.

HILDA.

I suppose she is very chilly by nature?

SOLNESS.

She is. And as we drove home, we were to see the smoke.

HILDA.

Only the smoke?

SOLNESS.

The smoke first. But when we came up to the garden gate, the whole of the old timber-box was to be a rolling mass of flames.—That is how I wanted it to be, you see.

HILDA.

Oh why, why could it not have happened so!

SOLNESS.

You may well say that, Hilda.

HILDA.

Well, but now listen, Mr. Solness. Are you perfectly certain that the fire was caused by that little crack in the chimney!

SOLNESS.

No, on the contrary—I am perfectly certain that the crack in the chimney had nothing whatever to do with the fire.

HILDA.

What!

SOLNESS.

It has been clearly ascertained that the fire broke out in a clothes-cupboard—in a totally different part of the house.

HILDA.

Then what is all this nonsense you are talking about the crack in the chimney!

SOLNESS.

May I go on talking to you a little, Hilda?

HILDA.

Yes, if you'll only talk sensibly——

SOLNESS.

I will try to. [*He moves his chair nearer.*

HILDA.

Out with it, then, Mr. Solness.

SOLNESS.

[*Confidentially.*] Don't you agree with me, Hilda, that there exist special, chosen people who have been endowed with the power and faculty of desiring a thing, craving for a thing, willing a thing—so persistently and so—so inexorably—that at last it has to happen? Don't you believe that?

HILDA.

[*With an indefinable expression in her eyes.*] It that is so, we shall see, one of these days, whether *I* am one of the chosen.

SOLNESS.

It is not one's self alone that can do such great things. Oh, no—the helpers and the servers—they must do their part too, if it is to be of any good. But they never come of themselves. One has to call upon them very persistently—inwardly, you understand.

HILDA.

What are these helpers and servers?

SOLNESS.

Oh, we can talk about that some other time. For the present, let us keep to this business of the fire.

HILDA.

Don't you think that fire would have happened all the same—even without your wishing for it?

SOLNESS.

If the house had been old Knut Brovik's, it would never have burnt down so conveniently for him. I am sure of that; for he does not know how to call for the helpers—no, nor for the servers, either. [*Rises in unrest*] So you see, Hilda—it is my fault, after all, that the lives of the two little boys had to be sacrificed. And do you think it is not my fault, too, that Aline has never been the woman she should and might have been—and that she most longed to be?

HILDA.

Yes, but if it is all the work of those helpers and servers——?

SOLNESS.

Who called for the helpers and servers? It was I! And they came and obeyed my will. [*In increasing excitement.*] That is what people call having the luck on your side; but I must tell you what this sort of luck feels like! It feels like a great raw place here on my breast. And the helpers and servers keep on flaying pieces of skin off other people in order to close my sore! —But still the sore is not healed—never, never! Oh, if you knew how it can sometimes gnaw and burn

HILDA.

[*Looks attentively at him.*] You are ill, Mr. Solness. Very ill, I almost think.

SOLNESS.

Say mad; for that is what you mean.

HILDA.

No, I don't think there is much amiss with your intellect.

SOLNESS.

With what then? Out with it!

HILDA.

I wonder whether you were not sent into the world with a sickly conscience.

SOLNESS.

A sickly conscience? What devilry is that?

HILDA.

I mean that your conscience is feeble—too delicately built, as it were—hasn't strength to take a grip of things—to lift and bear what is heavy.

SOLNESS.

[*Growls.*] H'm! May I ask, then, what sort of a conscience one ought to have?

HILDA.

I should like your conscience to be—to be thoroughly robust.

SOLNESS.

Indeed? Robust, eh? Is your own conscience robust, may I ask?

HILDA.

Yes, I think it is. I have never noticed that it wasn't.

SOLNESS.

It has not been put very severely to the test, I should think.

HILDA.

[*With a quivering of the lips.*] Oh, it was no such simple matter to leave father—I am so awfully fond of him.

SOLNESS.

Dear me! for a month or two——

HILDA.

I think I shall never go home again.

SOLNESS.

Never? Then why did you leave him?

HILDA.

[*Half-seriously, half-banteringly.*] Have you forgotten again that the ten years are up?

SOLNESS.

Oh nonsense. Was anything wrong at home? Eh?

HILDA.

[*Quite seriously.*] It was this impulse within me that urged and goaded me to come—and lured and drew me on, as well.

SOLNESS.

[*Eagerly.*] There we have it! There we have it, Hilda! There is a troll in you too, as in me. For it's the troll in one, you see—it is that that calls to the powers outside us. And then you must give in—whether you will or no.

HILDA.

I almost think you are right, Mr. Solness.

SOLNESS.

[*Walks about the room.*] Oh, there are devils innumerable abroad in the world, Hilda, that one never sees!

HILDA.

Devils, too?

SOLNESS.

[*Stops.*] Good devils and bad devils; light-haired devils and black-haired devils. If only you could always tell whether it is the light or dark ones that have got hold of you! [*Paces about.*] Ho-ho! Then it would be simple enough!

HILDA.

[*Follows him with her eyes.*] Or if one had a really vigorous, radiantly healthy conscience—so that one dared to do what one would.

SOLNESS.

[*Stops beside the console table.*] I believe, now, that most people are just as puny creatures as I am in that respect.

HILDA.

I shouldn't wonder.

SOLNESS.

[*Leaning against the table.*] In the sagas——. Have you read any of the old sagas?

HILDA.

Oh yes! When I used to read books, I——

SOLNESS

In the sagas you read about vikings, who sailed to foreign lands, and plundered and burned and killed men——

HILDA.

And carried off women——

SOLNESS.

——and kept them in captivity——

HILDA.

——took them home in their ships——

SOLNESS.

——and behaved to them like—like the very worst of trolls.

HILDA.

[*Looks straight before her, with a half-veiled look.*] I think that must have been thrilling.

SOLNESS.

[*With a short, deep laugh.*] To carry off women eh?

HILDA.

To be carried off.

SOLNESS.

[*Looks at her a moment.*] Oh, indeed.

HILDA.

[*As if breaking the thread of the conversation.*] But what made you speak of these vikings, Mr. Solness?

SOLNESS.

Why, those fellows must have had robust consciences, if you like! When they got home again, they could eat and drink, and be as happy as children. And the women, too! They often would not leave them on any account. Can you understand that, Hilda?

HILDA

Those women I can understand exceedingly well.

SOLNESS.

Oho! Perhaps you could do the same yourself?

HILDA.

Why not?

SOLNESS.

Live—of your own free will—with a ruffian like that?

HILDA.

If it was a ruffian I had come to love——

SOLNESS.

Could you come to love a man like that?

HILDA.

Good heavens, you know very well one can't choose whom one is going to love.

SOLNESS.

[*Looks meditatively at her.*] Oh no, I suppose it is the troll within one that's responsible for that.

HILDA.

[*Half-laughing.*] And all those blessëd devils, that you know so well—both the light-haired and the dark-haired ones.

SOLNESS.

[*Quietly and warmly.*] Then I hope with all my heart that the devils will choose carefully for you, Hilda.

HILDA.

For me they have chosen already—once and for all.

SOLNESS.

[*Looks earnestly at her.*] Hilda—you are like a wild bird of the woods.

HILDA.

Far from it. I don't hide myself away under the bushes.

SOLNESS.

No, no. There is rather something of the bird of prey in you.

HILDA.

That is nearer it—perhaps. [*Very vehemently.*] And why not a bird of prey? Why should not *I* go a-hunting—I, as well as the rest? Carry off the prey I want—if only I can get my claws into it, and do with it as I will.

SOLNESS.

Hilda—do you know what you are?

HILDA.

Yes, I suppose I am a strange sort of bird.

SOLNESS.

No. You are like a dawning day. When I look at you—I seem to be looking towards the sunrise.

HILDA.

Tell me, Mr. Solness—are you certain that you have never called me to you? Inwardly, you know?

SOLNESS.

[*Softly and slowly.*] I almost think I must have.

HILDA.

What did you want with me?

SOLNESS.

You are the younger generation, Hilda.

HILDA.

[*Smiles.*] That younger generation that you are so afraid of?

SOLNESS.

[*Nods slowly.*] And which, in my heart, I yearn towards so deeply.

[HILDA *rises, goes to the little table, and fetches* RAGNAR BROVIK'S *portfolio.*

HILDA.

[*Holds out the portfolio to him.*] We were talking of these drawings——

SOLNESS.

[*Shortly, waving them away.*] Put those things away! I have seen enough of them.

HILDA.

Yes, but you have to write your approval on them.

SOLNESS.

Write my approval on them? Never!

HILDA.

But the poor old man is lying at death's door! Can't you give him and his son this pleasure before they are parted? And perhaps he might get the commission to carry them out, too.

SOLNESS.

Yes, that is just what he would get. He has made sure of that—has my fine gentleman!

HILDA.

Then, good heavens—if that is so—can't you tell the least little bit of a lie for once in a way?

SOLNESS.

A lie? [*Raging.*] Hilda—take those devil's drawings out of my sight!

HILDA.

[*Draws the portfolio a little nearer to herself.*] Well well, well—don't bite me.—You talk of trolls—but I think you go on like a troll yourself. [*Looks round.*] Where do you keep your pen and ink?

SOLNESS.

There is nothing of the sort in here.

HILDA.

[*Goes towards the door.*] But in the office where that young lady is——

SOLNESS.

Stay where you are, Hilda!—I ought to tell a lie, you say. Oh yes, for the sake of his old father I might well do that—for in my time I have crushed him, trodden him under foot——

HILDA.

Him, too?

SOLNESS.

I needed room for myself. But this Ragnar—he must on no account be allowed to come to the front.

HILDA.

Poor fellow, there is surely no fear of that. If he has nothing in him——

SOLNESS.

[*Comes closer, looks at her, and whispers.*] If Ragnar Brovik gets his chance, he will strike me to the earth. Crush me—as I crushed his father.

HILDA.

Crush you? Has he the ability for that?

SOLNESS.

Yes, you may depend upon it he has the ability! He is the younger generation that stands ready to knock at my door—to make an end of Halvard Solness.

HILDA.

[*Looks at him with quiet reproach.*] And yet you would bar him out. Fie, Mr. Solness!

SOLNESS.

The fight I have been fighting has cost heart's blood enough.—And I am afraid, too, that the helpers and servers will not obey me any longer.

HILDA.

Then you must go ahead without them. There is nothing else for it.

SOLNESS.

It is hopeless, Hilda. The luck is bound to turn. A little sooner or a little later. Retribution is inexorable.

HILDA.

[*In distress, putting her hands over her ears.*] Don't talk like that! Do you want to kill me? To take from me what is more than my life?

SOLNESS.

And what is that?

HILDA.

The longing to see you great. To see you, with a wreath in your hand, high, high up upon a church-tower. [*Calm again.*] Come, out with your pencil now. You must have a pencil about you?

SOLNESS.

[*Takes out his pocket-book.*] I have one here.

HILDA.

[*Lays the portfolio on the sofa-table.*] Very well. Now let us two sit down here, Mr. Solness. [SOLNESS *seats himself at the table.* HILDA *stands behind him, leaning over the back of the chair.*] And now we will write on the drawings. We must write very, very nicely and cordially—for this horrid Ruar—or whatever his name is.

SOLNESS.

[*Writes a few words, turns his head and looks at her.*] Tell me one thing, Hilda.

HILDA.

Yes!

SOLNESS.

If you have been waiting for me all these ten years——

HILDA.

What then?

SOLNESS.

Why have you never written to me? Then I could have answered you.

HILDA.

[*Hastily.*] No, no, no! That was just what I did not want.

SOLNESS.

Why not?

HILDA.

I was afraid the whole thing might fall to pieces.—But we were going to write on the drawings, Mr. Solness.

SOLNESS.

So we were.

HILDA.

[*Bends forward and looks over his shoulder while he writes.*] Mind now, kindly and cordially! Oh how I hate—how I hate this Ruald——

SOLNESS.

[*Writing.*] Have you never really cared for any one, Hilda?

HILDA.

[*Harshly.*] What do you say?

SOLNESS.

Have you never cared for any one?

HILDA.

For any one else, I suppose you mean?

SOLNESS.

[*Looks up at her.*] For any one else, yes. Have you never? In all these ten years? Never?

HILDA.

Oh yes, now and then. When I was perfectly furious with you for not coming.

SOLNESS.

Then you did take an interest in other people, too?

HILDA.

A little bit—for a week or so. Good heavens, Mr. Solness, you surely know how such things come about.

SOLNESS.

Hilda—what is it you have come for?

HILDA.

Don't waste time talking. The poor old man might go and die in the meantime.

SOLNESS.

Answer me Hilda. What do you want of me?

HILDA.

I want my kingdom.

SOLNESS.

H'm——

He gives a rapid glance towards the door on the left, and then goes on writing on the drawings. At the same moment MRS. SOLNESS *enters; she has some packages in her hand.*

MRS. SOLNESS.

Here are a few things I have got for you, Miss Wangel. The large parcels will be sent later on.

HILDA.

Oh, how very, very kind of you!

MRS. SOLNESS.

Only my simple duty. Nothing more than that.

SOLNESS.

[*Reading over what he has written.*] Aline!

MRS. SOLNESS.

Yes?

SOLNESS.

Did you notice whether the—the book-keeper was out there?

MRS. SOLNESS.

Yes, of course, she was there.

SOLNESS.

[*Puts the drawings in the portfolio.*] H'm——

MRS. SOLNESS.

She was standing at the desk, as she always is —when *I* go through the room.

SOLNESS.

[*Rises.*] Then I'll give this to her, and tell her that——

HILDA.

[*Takes the portfolio from him.*] Oh, no, let me have the pleasure of doing that! [*Goes to the door, but turns.*] What is her name?

SOLNESS.

Her name is Miss Fosli.

HILDA.

Pooh, that sounds so cold! Her Christian name, I mean?

SOLNESS.

Kaia—I believe.

HILDA.

[*Opens the door and calls out.*] Kaia, come in here! Make haste! Mr. Solness wants to speak to you.

KAIA FOSLI *appears at the door.*

KAIA.

[*Looking at him in alarm.*] Here I am——?

HILDA.

[*Handing her the portfolio.*] See here, Kaia! You can take this home; Mr. Solness has written on them now.

KAIA.

Oh, at last!

SOLNESS.

Give them to the old man as soon as you can.

KAIA.

I will go straight home with them.

SOLNESS.

Yes, do. Now Ragnar will have a chance of building for himself.

KAIA.

Oh, may he come and thank you for all——?

SOLNESS.

[*Harshly.*] I won't have any thanks! Tell him that from me.

KAIA.

Yes, I will——

SOLNESS.

And tell him at the same time that henceforward I do not require his services—nor yours either.

KAIA.

[*Softly and quiveringly.*] Not mine either?

SOLNESS.

You will have other things to think of now, and to attend to; and that is a very good thing for you. Well, go home with the drawings now, Miss Fosli. At once! Do you hear?

KAIA.

[*As before.*] Yes, Mr. Solness. [*She goes out.*

MRS. SOLNESS.

Heavens! what deceitful eyes she has.

SOLNESS.

She? That poor little creature?

MRS. SOLNESS.

Oh—I can see what I can see, Halvard.—— Are you really dismissing them?

SOLNESS.

Yes.

MRS. SOLNESS.

Her as well?

SOLNESS.

Was not that what you wished?

MRS. SOLNESS.

But how can you get on without her——? Oh well, no doubt you have some one else in reserve, Halvard.

HILDA.

[*Playfully.*] Well, *I* for one am not the person to stand at that desk.

SOLNESS.

Never mind, never mind—it will be all right, Aline. Now all you have to do is to think about moving into our new home—as quickly as you can. This evening we will hang up the wreath—[*Turns to* HILDA]—right on the very pinnacle of the tower. What do you say to that, Miss Hilda?

HILDA.

[*Looks at him with sparkling eyes.*] It will be splendid to see you so high up once more.

SOLNESS.

Me!

MRS. SOLNESS.

For Heaven's sake, Miss Wangel, don't imagine such a thing! My husband!—when he always gets so dizzy!

HILDA.

He get dizzy! No, I know quite well he does not!

MRS. SOLNESS.

Oh yes, indeed he does.

HILDA.

But I have seen him with my own eyes right up at the top of a high church-tower!

MRS. SOLNESS.

Yes, I hear people talk of that; but it is utterly impossible——

SOLNESS.

[*Vehemently.*] Impossible—impossible, yes! But there I stood all the same!

MRS. SOLNESS.

Oh, how can you say so, Halvard? Why, you can't even bear to go out on the second-storey balcony here. You have always been like that.

SOLNESS.

You may perhaps see something different this evening.

MRS. SOLNESS.

[*In alarm.*] No, no, no! Please God I shall never see that. I will write at once to the doctor—and I am sure he won't let you do it.

SOLNESS.

Why, Aline——!

MRS. SOLNESS.

Oh, you know you're ill, Halvard. This proves it! Oh God—Oh God!

[*She goes hastily out to the right.*

HILDA.

[*Looks intently at him.*] Is it so, or is it not?

SOLNESS.

That I turn dizzy?

HILDA.

That my master builder dares not—cannot—climb as high as he builds?

SOLNESS.

Is that the way you look at it?

HILDA.

Yes.

SOLNESS.

I believe there is scarcely a corner in me that is safe from you.

HILDA.

[*Looks towards the bow-window.*] Up there, then. Right up there——

SOLNESS.

[*Approaches her.*] You might have the topmost room in the tower, Hilda—there you might live like a princess.

HILDA.

[*Indefinably, between earnest and jest.*] Yes, that is what you promised me.

SOLNESS.

Did I really?

HILDA.

Fie, Mr. Solness! You said I should be a princess, and that you would give me a kingdom. And then you went and——Well!

SOLNESS.

[*Cautiously.*] Are you quite certain that this is not a dream—a fancy, that has fixed itself in your mind?

HILDA.

[*Sharply.*] Do you mean that you did not do it?

SOLNESS.

I scarcely know myself. [*More softly.*] But now I know so much for certain, that I——

HILDA.

That you——? Say it at once!

SOLNESS.

——that I ought to have done it.

HILDA.

[*Exclaims with animation.*] Don't tell me you can ever be dizzy!

SOLNESS.

This evening, then, we will hang up the wreath—Princess Hilda.

HILDA.

[*With a bitter curve of the lips.*] Over your new home, yes.

SOLNESS.

Over the new house, which will never be a home for me.

[*He goes out through the garden door.*

HILDA.

[*Looks straight in front of her with a far-away expression, and whispers to herself. The only words audible are*]——frightfully thrilling——

ACT THIRD.

The large, broad verandah of SOLNESS'S *dwelling-house. Part of the house, with outer door leading to the verandah, is seen to the left. A railing along the verandah to the right. At the back, from the end of the verandah, a flight of steps leads down to the garden below. Tall old trees in the garden spread their branches over the verandah and towards the house. Far to the right, in among the trees, a glimpse is caught of the lower part of the new villa, with scaffolding round so much as is seen of the tower. In the background the garden is bounded by an old wooden fence. Outside the fence, a street with low, tumble-down cottages.*

Evening sky with sun-lit clouds.

On the verandah, a garden bench stands along the wall of the house, and in front of the bench a long table. On the other side of the table, an arm-chair and some stools. All the furniture is of wicker-work.

MRS. SOLNESS, *wrapped in a large white crape shawl, sits resting in the arm-chair and gazes over to the right. Shortly after,* HILDA WANGEL *comes up the flight of steps from the garden. She is dressed as in the last act, and wears her hat. She has in her bodice a little nosegay of small common flowers.*

MRS. SOLNESS.

[*Turning her head a little.*] Have you been round the garden, Miss Wangel?

HILDA.

Yes, I have been taking a look at it.

MRS. SOLNESS.

And found some flowers too, I see.

HILDA.

Yes, indeed! There are such heaps of them in among the bushes.

MRS. SOLNESS.

Are there really? Still? You see I scarcely ever go there.

HILDA.

[*Closer.*] What! Don't you take a run down into the garden every day, then?

MRS. SOLNESS.

[*With a faint smile.*] I don't "run" anywhere, nowadays.

HILDA.

Well, but do you not go down now and then to look at all the lovely things there?

MRS. SOLNESS.

It has all become so strange to me I am almost afraid to see it again.

HILDA.

Your own garden!

MRS. SOLNESS.

I don't feel that it is mine any longer.

HILDA.

What do you mean——?

MRS. SOLNESS.

No, no, it is not—not as it was in my mother's and father's time. They have taken away so much—so much of the garden, Miss Wangel. Fancy—they have parcelled it out—and built houses for strangers—people that I don't know. And they can sit and look in upon me from their windows.

HILDA.

[*With a bright expression.*] Mrs. Solness!

MRS. SOLNESS.

Yes!

HILDA.

May I stay here with you a little?

MRS. SOLNESS.

Yes, by all means, if you care to.

[HILDA *moves a stool close to the arm-chair and sits down.*

HILDA.

Ah—here one can sit and sun oneself like a cat.

MRS. SOLNESS.

[*Lays her hand softly on* HILDA's *neck.*] It is nice of you to be willing to sit with me. I thought you wanted to go in to my husband.

HILDA.

What should I want with him?

MRS. SOLNESS.

To help him, I thought.

HILDA.

No, thank you. And besides, he is not in. He is over there with his workmen. But he looked so fierce that I did not dare to talk to him.

MRS. SOLNESS.

He is so kind and gentle in reality.

HILDA.

He!

MRS. SOLNESS.

You do not really know him yet, Miss Wangel.

HILDA.

[*Looks affectionately at her.*] Are you pleased at the thought of moving over to the new house?

MRS. SOLNESS.

I ought to be pleased; for it is what Halvard wants——

HILDA.

Oh, not just on that account, surely.

MRS. SOLNESS.

Yes, yes, Miss Wangel; for it is only my duty to submit myself to him. But very often it is dreadfully difficult to force one's mind to obedience.

HILDA.

Yes, that must be difficult indeed.

MRS. SOLNESS.

I can tell you it is—when one has so many faults as I have——

HILDA.

When one has gone through so much trouble as you have——

MRS. SOLNESS.

How do you know about that?

HILDA.

Your husband told me.

MRS. SOLNESS.

To me he very seldom mentions these things.—Yes, I can tell you I have gone through more than enough trouble in my life, Miss Wangel.

HILDA.

[*Looks sympathetically at her and nods slowly.*] Poor Mrs. Solness. First of all there was the fire——

MRS. SOLNESS.

[*With a sigh.*] Yes, everything that was mine was burnt.

HILDA.

And then came what was worse.

MRS. SOLNESS.

[*Looking inquiringly at her.*] Worse?

HILDA.

The worst of all.

MRS. SOLNESS.

What do you mean?

HILDA.

[*Softly.*] You lost the two little boys.

MRS. SOLNESS.

Oh yes, the boys. But, you see, that was a thing apart. That was a dispensation of Providence; and in such things one can only bow in submission—yes, and be thankful, too.

HILDA.

Then you are so?

MRS. SOLNESS.

Not always, I am sorry to say. I know well enough that it is my duty—but all the same I cannot.

HILDA.

No, no, I think that is only natural.

MRS. SOLNESS.

And often and often I have to remind myself that it was a righteous punishment for me——

HILDA.

Why?

MRS. SOLNESS.

Because I had not fortitude enough in misfortune.

HILDA.

But I don't see that——

MRS. SOLNESS.

Oh, no, no, Miss Wangel—do not talk to me any more about the two little boys. We ought to feel nothing but joy in thinking of them; for they are so happy—so happy now. No, it is the small losses in life that cut one to the heart—the loss of all that other people look upon as almost nothing.

HILDA.

[*Lays her arms on* MRS. SOLNESS'S *knees, and looks up at her affectionately.*] Dear Mrs. Solness—tell me what things you mean!

MRS. SOLNESS.

As I say, only little things. All the old portraits were burnt on the walls. And all the old silk dresses were burnt, that had belonged to the family for generations and generations. And all mother's and grandmother's lace—that was burnt, too. And only think—the jewels, too! [*Sadly.*] And then all the dolls.

HILDA.

The dolls?

MRS. SOLNESS.

[*Choking with tears.*] I had nine lovely dolls.

HILDA.

And they were burnt too?

MRS. SOLNESS.

All of them. Oh, it was hard—so hard for me.

HILDA.

Had you put by all these dolls, then? Ever since you were little?

MRS. SOLNESS.

I had not put them by. The dolls and I had gone on living together.

HILDA.

After you were grown up?

MRS. SOLNESS.

Yes, long after that.

HILDA.

After you were married, too?

MRS. SOLNESS.

Oh yes, indeed. So long as he did not see it——. But they were all burnt up, poor things. No one thought of saving *them*. Oh, it is so miserable to think of. You mustn't laugh at me, Miss Wangel.

HILDA.

I am not laughing in the least.

MRS. SOLNESS.

For you see, in a certain sense, there was life in them, too. I carried them under my heart—like little unborn children.

DR. HERDAL, *with his hat in his hand, comes out through the door, and observes* MRS. SOLNESS *and* HILDA.

DR. HERDAL.

Well, Mrs. Solness, so you are sitting out here catching cold?

MRS. SOLNESS.

I find it so pleasant and warm here to-day.

DR. HERDAL.

Yes, yes. But is there anything going on here? I got a note from you.

MRS. SOLNESS.

[*Rises.*] Yes, there is something I must talk to you about.

DR. HERDAL.

Very well; then perhaps we had better go in. [*To* HILDA.] Still in your mountaineering dress, Miss Wangel?

HILDA.

[*Gaily, rising.*] Yes—in full uniform! But to-day I am not going climbing and breaking my neck. We two will stop quietly below and look on, doctor.

DR. HERDAL.

What are we to look on at?

MRS. SOLNESS.

[*Softly, in alarm, to* HILDA.] Hush, hush—for God's sake! He is coming! Try to get that idea out of his head. And let us be friends, Miss Wangel. Don't you think we can?

HILDA.

[*Throws her arms impetuously round* MRS. SOLNESS'S *neck.*] Oh, if we only could!

MRS. SOLNESS.

[*Gently disengages herself.*] There, there, there! There he comes, doctor. Let me have a word with you.

DR. HERDAL.

Is it about him!

MRS. SOLNESS.

Yes, to be sure it's about him. Do come in.

She and the doctor enter the house. Next moment SOLNESS *comes up from the garden by the flight of steps. A serious look comes over* HILDA'S *face.*

SOLNESS.

[*Glances at the house-door, which is closed cautiously from within.*] Have you noticed, Hilda, that as soon as I come, she goes?

HILDA.

I have noticed that as soon as you come, you make her go.

SOLNESS.

Perhaps so. But I cannot help it. [*Looks observantly at her.*] Are you cold, Hilda? I think you look cold.

HILDA.

I have just come up out of a tomb.

SOLNESS.

What do you mean by that?

HILDA.

That I have got chilled through and through, Mr. Solness.

SOLNESS.

[*Slowly.*] I believe I understand——

HILDA.

What brings you up here just now?

SOLNESS.

I caught sight of you from over there.

HILDA.

But then you must have seen her too?

SOLNESS.

I knew she would go at once if I came.

HILDA.

Is it very painful for you that she should avoid you in this way?

SOLNESS.

In one sense, it's a relief as well.

HILDA.

Not to have her before your eyes?

SOLNESS.

Yes.

HILDA.

Not to be always seeing how heavily the loss of the little boys weighs upon her?

SOLNESS.

Yes. Chiefly that.

[HILDA *drifts across the verandah with her hands behind her back, stops at the railing and looks out over the garden.*

SOLNESS.

[*After a short pause.*] Did you have a long talk with her?

[HILDA *stands motionless and does not answer.*

SOLNESS.

Had you a long talk, I asked?

[HILDA *is silent as before.*

SOLNESS.

What was she talking about, Hilda?

[HILDA *continues silent.*

SOLNESS.

Poor Aline! I suppose it was about the little boys.

HILDA.

[*A nervous shudder runs through her; then she nods hurriedly once or twice.*

SOLNESS.

She will never get over it—never in this world. [*Approaches her.*] Now you are standing there again like a statue; just as you stood last night.

HILDA.

[*Turns and looks at him, with great serious eyes.*] I am going away.

SOLNESS.

[*Sharply.*] Going away!

HILDA.

Yes.

SOLNESS.

But I won't allow you to!

HILDA.

What am I to do here now?

SOLNESS.

Simply to be here, Hilda!

HILDA.

[*Measures him with a look.*] Oh, thank you. You know it wouldn't end there.

SOLNESS.

[*Heedlessly.*] So much the better!

HILDA.

[*Vehemently.*] I cannot do any harm to one whom I know! I can't take away anything that belongs to her.

SOLNESS.

Who wants you to do that?

HILDA.

[*Continuing.*] A stranger, yes! for that is quite a different thing! A person I have never set eyes on. But one that I have come into close contact with——! Oh no! Oh no! Ugh!

SOLNESS.

Yes, but I never proposed you should.

HILDA.

Oh, Mr. Solness, you know quite well what the end of it would be. And that is why I am going away.

SOLNESS.

And what is to become of me when you are gone? What shall I have to live for then?—After that?

HILDA.

[*With the indefinable look in her eyes.*] It is surely not so hard for you. You have your duties to her. Live for those duties.

SOLNESS.

Too late. These powers—these—these——

HILDA.

——devils——

SOLNESS.

Yes, these devils! And the troll within me as well—they have drawn all the life-blood out of her. [*Laughs in desperation.*] They did it for my happiness! Yes, yes! [*Sadly.*] And now she is dead—for my sake. And I am chained alive to a dead woman. [*In wild anguish.*] *I—I* who cannot live without joy in life!

[HILDA *moves round the table and seats herself on the bench, with her elbows on the table, and her head supported by her hands.*

HILDA.

[*Sits and looks at him awhile.*] What will you build next?

SOLNESS.

[*Shakes his head.*] I don't believe I shall build much more.

HILDA.

Not those cosy, happy homes for mother and father, and for the troop of children?

SOLNESS.

I wonder whether there will be any use for such homes in the coming time.

HILDA.

Poor Mr. Solness! And you have gone all these ten years—and staked your whole life—on that alone.

SOLNESS.

Yes, you may well say so, Hilda.

HILDA.

[*With an outburst.*] Oh, it all seems to me so foolish—so foolish!

SOLNESS.

All what?

HILDA.

Not to be able to grasp at your own happiness—at your own life! Merely because some one you know happens to stand in the way!

SOLNESS.

One whom you have no right to set aside.

HILDA.

I wonder whether one really has not the right! And yet, and yet——. Oh! if one could only sleep the whole thing away!

[*She lays her arms flat down on the table, rests the left side of her head on her hands, and shuts her eyes.*

SOLNESS.

[*Turns the arm-chair and sits down at the table.*] Had you a cosy, happy home—up there with your father, Hilda?

HILDA.

[*Without stirring, answers as if half asleep.*] I had only a cage.

SOLNESS.

And you are determined not to go back to it?

HILDA

[*As before.*] The wild bird never wants to go into the cage.

SOLNESS.

Rather range through the free air——

HILDA.

[*Still as before.*] The bird of prey loves to range——

SOLNESS.

[*Lets his eyes rest on her.*] If only one had the viking-spirit in life——

HILDA.

[*In her usual voice; opens her eyes but does not move.*] And the other thing? Say what that was!

SOLNESS.

A robust conscience.

[HILDA *sits erect on the bench, with animation. Her eyes have once more the sparkling expression of gladness.*

HILDA.

[*Nods to him.*] *I* know what you are going to build next!

SOLNESS.

Then you know more than I do, Hilda.

HILDA.

Yes, builders are such stupid people.

SOLNESS.

What is it to be then?

HILDA.

[*Nods again.*] The castle.

SOLNESS.

What castle?

HILDA.

My castle, of course.

SOLNESS.

Do you want a castle now?

HILDA.

Don't you owe me a kingdom, I should like to know?

SOLNESS.

You say I do.

HILDA.

Well—you admit you owe me this kingdom. And you can't have a kingdom without a royal castle, I should think!

SOLNESS.

[*More and more animated.*] Yes, they usually go together.

HILDA.

Good! Then build it for me! This moment!

SOLNESS.

[*Laughing.*] Must you have that on the instant, too?

HILDA.

Yes, to be sure! For the ten years are up now, and I am not going to wait any longer. So—out with the castle, Mr. Solness!

SOLNESS.

It's no light matter to owe *you* anything, Hilda.

HILDA.

You should have thought of that before. It is too late now. So—[*tapping the table*]—the castle on the table! It is *my* castle! I will have it *at once*!

SOLNESS.

[*More seriously, leans over towards her, with his arms on the table.*] What sort of castle have you imagined, Hilda?

[*Her expression becomes more and more veiled. She seems gazing inwards at herself.*

HILDA.

[*Slowly.*] My castle shall stand on a height—on a very great height—with a clear outlook on all sides, so that I can see far—far around.

SOLNESS.

And no doubt it is to have a high tower!

HILDA.

A tremendously high tower. And at the very top of the tower there shall be a balcony. And I will stand out upon it——

SOLNESS.

[*Involuntarily clutches at his forehead.*] How can you like to stand at such a dizzy height——?

HILDA.

Yes, I will! Right up there will I stand and look down on the other people—on those that are building churches, and homes for mother and father and the troop of children. And you may come up and look on at it, too.

SOLNESS.

[*In a low tone.*] Is the builder to be allowed to come up beside the princess?

HILDA.

If the builder will.

SOLNESS.

[*More softly.*] Then I think the builder will come.

HILDA.

[*Nods.*] The builder—he will come.

SOLNESS.

But he will never be able to build any more. Poorbuilder!

HILDA.

[*Animated.*] Oh yes, he will! We two will set to work together. And then we will build the loveliest—the very loveliest—thing in all the world.

SOLNESS.

[*Intently.*] Hilda—tell me what that is!

HILDA.

[*Looks smilingly at him, shakes her head a little, pouts, and speaks as if to a child.*] Builders—they are such very—very stupid people.

SOLNESS.

Yes, no doubt they are stupid. But now tell me what it is—the loveliest thing in the world—that we two are to build together?

HILDA.

[*Is silent a little while, then says with an indefinable expression in her eyes.*] Castles in the air.

SOLNESS.

Castles in the air?

HILDA.

[*Nods.*] Castles in the air, yes! Do you know what sort of thing a castle in the air is?

SOLNESS.

It is the loveliest thing in the world, you say.

HILDA.

[*Rises with vehemence, and makes a gesture of repulsion with her hand.*] Yes, to be sure it is! Castles in the air—they are so easy to take refuge in. And so easy to build, too—[*looks scornfully at him*]—especially for the builders who have a—a dizzy conscience.

SOLNESS.

[*Rises.*] After this day we two will build together, Hilda.

HILDA.

[*With a half-dubious smile.*] A real castle in the air?

SOLNESS.

Yes. One with a firm foundation under it.

RAGNAR BROVIK *comes out from the house. He is carrying a large, green wreath with flowers and silk ribbons.*

HILDA.

[*With an outburst of pleasure.*] The wreath! Oh, that will be glorious!

SOLNESS.

[*In surprise.*] Have you brought the wreath Ragnar?

RAGNAR.

I promised the foreman I would.

SOLNESS.

[*Relieved.*] Ah, then I suppose your father is better?

RAGNAR.

No.

SOLNESS.

Was he not cheered by what I wrote?

RAGNAR.

It came too late.

SOLNESS.

Too late!

RAGNAR.

When she came with it he was unconscious. He had had a stroke.

SOLNESS.

Why, then, you must go home to him! You must attend to your father!

RAGNAR.

He does not need me any more.

SOLNESS.

But surely you ought to be with him

RAGNAR.

She is sitting by his bed.

SOLNESS.

[*Rather uncertainly.*] Kaia?

RAGNAR.

[*Looking darkly at him.*] Yes—Kaia

SOLNESS.

Go home, Ragnar—both to him and to her. Give me the wreath.

RAGNAR.

[*Suppresses a mocking smile.*] You don't mean that you yourself——?

SOLNESS.

I will take it down to them myself. [*Takes the wreath from him.*] And now you go home; we don't require you to-day.

RAGNAR.

I know you do not require me any more; but to-day I shall remain.

SOLNESS.

Well, remain then, since you are bent upon it.

HILDA.

[*At the railing.*] Mr. Solness, I will stand here and look on at you.

SOLNESS.

At me!

HILDA.

It will be fearfully thrilling.

SOLNESS.

[*In a low tone.*] We will talk about that presently, Hilda.

[*He goes down the flight of steps with the wreath, and away through the garden.*

HILDA.

[*Looks after him, then turns to* RAGNAR.] I think you might at least have thanked him.

RAGNAR.

Thanked him? Ought I to have thanked him?

HILDA.

Yes, of course you ought!

RAGNAR.

I think it is rather you I ought to thank.

HILDA.

How can you say such a thing?

RAGNAR.

[*Without answering her.*] But I advise you to take care, Miss Wangel! For you don't know him rightly yet.

HILDA.

[*Ardently.*] Oh, no one knows him as I do!

RAGNAR.

[*Laughs in exasperation.*] Thank him, when he has held me down year after year! When he made father disbelieve in me—made me disbelieve in myself! And all merely that he might——!

HILDA.

[*As if divining something.*] That he might——? Tell me at once!

RAGNAR.

That he might keep her with him.

HILDA.

[*With a start towards him.*] The girl at the desk.

RAGNAR.

Yes.

HILDA.

[*Threateningly, clenching her hands.*] That is not true! You are telling falsehoods about him!

RAGNAR.

I would not believe it either until to-day—when she said so herself.

HILDA.

[*As if beside herself.*] What did she say? I will know! At once! at once!

RAGNAR.

She said that he had taken possession of her mind—her whole mind—centred all her thoughts upon himself alone. She says that she can never leave him—that she will remain here, where he is——

HILDA.

[*With flashing eyes.*] She will not be allowed to!

RAGNAR.

[*As if feeling his way.*] Who will not allow her?

HILDA.

[*Rapidly.*] He will not either!

RAGNAR.

Oh no—I understand the whole thing now. After this, she would merely be—in the way.

HILDA.

You understand nothing—since you can talk like that! No, *I* will tell you why he kept hold of her.

RAGNAR.

Well then, why?

HILDA.

In order to keep hold of you.

RAGNAR.

Has he told you so?

HILDA.

No, but it is so. It must be so! [*Wildly.*] I will—I will have it so!

RAGNAR.

And at the very moment when you came—he let her go.

HILDA.

It was you—you that he let go! What do you suppose he cares about strange women like her?

RAGNAR.

[*Reflects.*] Is it possible that all this time he has been afraid of me?

HILDA.

He afraid! I would not be so conceited if I were you.

RAGNAR.

Oh, he must have seen long ago that I had something in me, too. Besides—cowardly—that is just what he is, you see.

HILDA.

He! Oh yes, I am likely to believe that!

RAGNAR.

In a certain sense he is cowardly—he, the great master builder. He is not afraid of robbing others of their life's happiness—as he has done both for my father and for me. But when it comes to climbing up a paltry bit of scaffolding—he will do anything rather than that.

HILDA.

Oh, you should just have seen him high, high up—at the dizzy height where I once saw him.

RAGNAR.

Did you see that?

HILDA.

Yes, indeed I did. How free and great he looked as he stood and fastened the wreath to the church vane!

RAGNAR.

I know that he ventured that, once in his life—one solitary time. It is a legend among us younger men. But no power on earth would induce him to do it again.

HILDA.

To-day he will do it again!

RAGNAR.

[*Scornfully.*] Yes, I daresay!

HILDA.

We shall see it!

RAGNAR.

That neither you nor I will see.

HILDA.

[*With uncontrollable vehemence.*] I will see it! I will and I must see it!

RAGNAR.

But he will not do it. He simply dare not do it. For you see he cannot get over this infirmity —master builder though he be.

MRS. SOLNESS *comes from the house on to the verandah.*

MRS. SOLNESS.

[*Looks around.*] Is he not here? Where has he gone to?

RAGNAR.

Mr. Solness is down with the men.

HILDA.

He took the wreath with him.

MRS. SOLNESS.

[*Terrified.*] Took the wreath with him! Oh God! oh God! Brovik—you must go down to him! Get him to come back here!

RAGNAR.

Shall I say you want to speak to him, Mrs. Solness?

MRS. SOLNESS.

Oh yes, do!—No, no—don't say that *I* want anything! You can say that somebody is here and that he must come at once.

RAGNAR.

Good. I will do so, Mrs. Solness.

[*He goes down the flight of steps and away through the garden.*

MRS. SOLNESS.

Oh, Miss Wangel, you can't think how anxious I feel about him.

HILDA.

Is there anything in this to be so terribly frightened about?

MRS. SOLNESS.

Oh yes; surely you can understand. Just think, if he were really to do it! If he should take it into his head to climb up the scaffolding!

HILDA.

[*Eagerly.*] Do you think he will?

MRS. SOLNESS.

Oh, one can never tell what he might take into his head. I am afraid there is nothing he mightn't think of doing.

HILDA.

Aha! Perhaps you too think that he is—well——?

MRS. SOLNESS.

Oh, I don't know what to think about him now. The doctor has been telling me all sorts of things; and putting it all together with several things I have heard him say——

DR. HERDAL *looks out, at the door.*

DR. HERDAL.

Is he not coming soon?

MRS. SOLNESS.

Yes, I think so. I have sent for him at any rate.

DR. HERDAL.

[*Advancing.*] I am afraid you will have to go in, my dear lady——

MRS. SOLNESS.

Oh no! Oh no! I shall stay out here and wait for Halvard.

DR. HERDAL.

But some ladies have just come to call on you——

MRS. SOLNESS.

Good heavens, *that* too! And just at this moment!

DR. HERDAL.

They say they positively must see the ceremony.

MRS. SOLNESS.

Well, well, I suppose I must go to them after all. It is my duty.

HILDA.

Can't you ask the ladies to go away?

MRS. SOLNESS.

No, that would never do. Now that they are here, it is my duty to see them. But do you stay out here in the meantime—and receive him when he comes.

DR. HERDAL.

And try to occupy his attention as long as possible——

MRS. SOLNESS.

Yes, do, dear Miss Wangel. Keep as firm hold of him as ever you can.

HILDA.

Would it not be best for you to do that?

MRS. SOLNESS.

Yes; God knows that is my duty. But when one has duties in so many directions——

DR. HERDAL.

[*Looks towards the garden.*] There he is coming.

MRS. SOLNESS.

And I have to go in!

DR. HERDAL.

[*To* HILDA.] Don't say anything about my being here.

HILDA.

Oh no! I daresay I shall find something else to talk to Mr. Solness about.

MRS. SOLNESS.

And be sure you keep firm hold of him. I believe you can do it best.

[MRS. SOLNESS *and* DR. HERDAL *go into the house.* HILDA *remains standing on the verandah.* SOLNESS *comes from the garden, up the flight of steps.*

SOLNESS.

Somebody wants me, I hear.

HILDA.

Yes; it is I, Mr. Solness.

SOLNESS.

Oh, is it you, Hilda? I was afraid it might be Aline or the Doctor.

HILDA.

You are very easily frightened, it seems!

SOLNESS.

Do you think so?

HILDA.

Yes; people say that you are afraid to climb about—on the scaffoldings, you know.

SOLNESS.

Well, that is quite a special thing.

HILDA.

Then it is true that you are afraid to do it?

SOLNESS.

Yes, I am.

HILDA.

Afraid of falling down and killing yourself?

SOLNESS.

No, not of that.

HILDA.

Of what, then?

SOLNESS.

I am afraid of retribution, Hilda.

HILDA.

Of retribution? [*Shakes her head.*] I don't understand that.

SOLNESS.

Sit down, and I will tell you something.

HILDA.

Yes, do! At once!

[*She sits on a stool by the railing, and looks expectantly at him.*

SOLNESS.

[*Throws his hat on the table.*] You know that I began by building churches.

HILDA.

[*Nods.*] I know that well.

SOLNESS.

For, you see, I came as a boy from a pious home in the country; and so it seemed to me that this church-building was the noblest task I could set myself.

HILDA.

Yes, yes.

SOLNESS.

And I venture to say that I built those poor little churches with such honest and warm and heartfelt devotion that—that——

HILDA.

That——? Well?

SOLNESS.

Well, that I think that he ought to have been pleased with me.

HILDA.

He? What he?

SOLNESS.

He who was to have the churches, of course! He to whose honour and glory they were dedicated.

HILDA.

Oh, indeed! But are you certain, then, that—that he was not—pleased with you?

SOLNESS.

[*Scornfully.*] He pleased with me! How can you talk so, Hilda? He who gave the troll in me leave to lord it just as it pleased. He who bade them be at hand to serve me, both day and night—all these—all these——

HILDA.

Devils——

SOLNESS.

Yes, of both kinds. Oh no, he made me feel clearly enough that he was not pleased with me. [*Mysteriously.*] You see, that was really the reason why he made the old house burn down.

HILDA.

Was that why?

SOLNESS.

Yes, don't you understand? He wanted to give me the chance of becoming an accomplished master in my own sphere—so that I might build all the more glorious churches for him. At first I did not understand what he was driving at; but all of a sudden it flashed upon me.

HILDA.

When was that?

SOLNESS.

It was when I was building the church-tower up at Lysanger.

HILDA.

I thought so.

SOLNESS.

For you see, Hilda—up there, amidst those new surroundings, I used to go about musing and pondering within myself. Then I saw plainly why he had taken my little children from me. It was that I should have nothing else to attach myself to. No such thing as love and happiness, you understand. I was to be only a master builder—nothing else. And all my life long I was to go on building for him. [*Laughs.*] But I can tell you nothing came of *that*!

HILDA.

What did you do, then?

SOLNESS.

First of all, I searched and tried my own heart——

HILDA.

And then?

SOLNESS.

Then I did the *impossible*—I no less than he.

HILDA.

The impossible?

SOLNESS.

I had never before been able to climb up to a great, free height. But that day I did it.

HILDA.

[*Leaping up.*] Yes, yes, you did!

SOLNESS.

And when I stood there, high over everything, and was hanging the wreath over the vane, I said to him: Hear me now, thou Mighty One! From this day forward I will be a free builder—I too, in my sphere—just as thou in thine. I will never more build churches for thee—only homes for human beings.

HILDA.

[*With great sparkling eyes.*] That was the song that I heard through the air!

SOLNESS.

But afterwards his turn came.

HILDA.

What do you mean by that?

SOLNESS.

[*Looks despondently at her.*] Building homes for human beings—is not worth a rap, Hilda.

HILDA.

Do you say that now?

SOLNESS.

Yes, for now I see it. Men have no use for these homes of theirs—to be happy in. And I should not have had any use for such a home, if I had had one. [*With a quiet, bitter laugh.*] See, that is the upshot of the whole affair, however far back I look. Nothing really built; nor anything sacrificed for the chance of building. Nothing, nothing! the whole is nothing!

HILDA.

Then you will never build anything more?

SOLNESS.

[*With animation.*] On the contrary, I am just going to begin!

HILDA.

What, then? What will you build? Tell me at once!

SOLNESS.

I believe there is only one possible dwelling-place for human happiness—and that is what I am going to build now.

HILDA.

[*Looks fixedly at him.*] Mr. Solness—you mean our castles in the air.

SOLNESS.

The castles in the air—yes.

HILDA.

I am afraid you would turn dizzy before we got half-way up.

SOLNESS.

Not if I can mount hand in hand with you, Hilda.

HILDA.

[*With an expression of suppressed resentment.*] Only with me? Will there be no others of the party?

SOLNESS.

Who else should there be?

HILDA.

Oh—that girl—that Kaia at the desk. Poor thing—don't you want to take her with you too?

SOLNESS.

Oho! Was it about her that Aline was talking to you?

HILDA.

Is it so—or is it not?

SOLNESS.

[*Vehemently.*] I will not answer such a question You must believe in me, wholly and entirely!

HILDA

All these ten years I have believed in you so utterly—so utterly.

SOLNESS.

You must go on believing in me!

HILDA.

Then let me see you stand free and high up!

SOLNESS.

[*Sadly.*] Oh Hilda—it is not every day that I can do that.

HILDA.

[*Passionately.*] I will have you do it! I will have it! [*Imploringly.*] Just once more, Mr. Solness! Do the impossible once again!

SOLNESS.

[*Stands and looks deep into her eyes.*] If I try it, Hilda, I will stand up there and talk to him as I did that time before.

HILDA.

[*In rising excitement.*] What will you say to him?

SOLNESS.

I will say to him: Hear me, Mighty Lord—thou may'st judge me as seems best to thee. But hereafter I will build nothing but the loveliest thing in the world——

HILDA.

[*Carried away.*] Yes—yes—yes!

SOLNESS.

—build it together with a princess, whom I love——

HILDA.

Yes, tell him that! Tell him that!

SOLNESS.

Yes. And then I will say to him: Now I shall go down and throw my arms round her and kiss her——

HILDA.

—many times! Say that!

SOLNESS.

—many, many times, I will say.

HILDA.

And then——?

SOLNESS.

Then I will wave my hat—and come down to the earth—and do as I said to him.

HILDA.

[*With outstretched arms.*] Now I see you again as I did when there was song in the air!

SOLNESS.

[*Looks at her with his head bowed.*] How have you become what you are, Hilda?

HILDA.

How have you made me what I am?

SOLNESS.

[*Shortly and firmly.*] The princess shall have her castle.

HILDA.

[*Jubilant, clapping her hands.*] Oh, Mr. Solness——! My lovely, lovely castle. Our castle in the air!

SOLNESS.

On a firm foundation.

[*In the street a crowd of people has assembled, vaguely seen through the trees. Music of wind-instruments is heard far away behind the new house.*

MRS. SOLNESS, *with a fur collar round her neck,* DOCTOR HERDAL *with her white shawl on his arm, and some ladies, come out on the verandah.* RAGNAR BROVIK *comes at the same time up from the garden.*

MRS. SOLNESS.

[*To* RAGNAR.] Are we to have music, too?

RAGNAR.

Yes. It's the band of the Mason's Union. [*To* SOLNESS.] The foreman asked me to tell you that he is ready now to go up with the wreath.

SOLNESS.

[*Takes his hat.*] Good. I will go down to him myself.

MRS. SOLNESS.

[*Anxiously.*] What have you to do down there, Halvard?

SOLNESS.

[*Curtly.*] I must be down below with the men.

MRS. SOLNESS.

Yes, down below—only down below.

SOLNESS.

That is where I always stand—on everyday occasions.

[*He goes down the flight of steps and away through the garden.*

MRS. SOLNESS.

[*Calls after him over the railing.*] But do beg the man to be careful when he goes up! Promise me that, Halvard!

DR. HERDAL.

[*To* MRS. SOLNESS.] Don't you see that I was right? He has given up all thought of that folly.

MRS. SOLNESS.

Oh, what a relief! Twice workmen have fallen, and each time they were killed on the spot. [*Turns to* HILDA.] Thank you, Miss Wangel, for having kept such a firm hold upon him. I should never have bee nable t omanage him.

DR. HERDAL.

[*Playfully*] Yes, yes, Miss Wangel, you know how to keep firm hold on a man, when you give your mind to it.

[MRS. SOLNESS *and* DR. HERDAL *go up to the ladies, who are standing nearer to the steps and looking over the garden.* HILDA *remains standing beside the railing in the foreground.* RAGNAR *goes up to her.*

RAGNAR.

[*With suppressed laughter, half whispering.*] Miss Wangel—do you see all those young fellows down in the street?

HILDA.

Yes.

RAGNAR.

They are my fellow students, come to look at the master.

HILDA.

What do they want to look at him for?

RAGNAR.

They want to see how he daren't climb to the top of his own house.

HILDA.

Oh, that is what those boys want, is it?

RAGNAR.

[*Spitefully and scornfully.*] He has kept us down so long—now we are going to see him keep quietly down below himself.

HILDA.

You will not see that—not this time.

RAGNAR.

[*Smiles.*] Indeed! Then where shall we see him?

HILDA.

High—high up by the vane! That is where you will see him!

RAGNAR.

[*Laughs.*] Him! Oh yes, I daresay!

HILDA.

His will is to reach the top—so at the top you shall see him.

RAGNAR.

His will, yes; that I can easily believe. But he simply cannot do it. His head would swim round, long, long before he got half-way. He would have to crawl down again on his hands and knees.

DR. HERDAL.

[*Points across.*] Look! There goes the foreman up the ladders.

MRS. SOLNESS.

And of course he has the wreath to carry too. Oh, I do hope he will be careful!

RAGNAR.

[*Stares incredulously and shouts.*] Why, but it's——

HILDA.

[*Breaking out in jubilation.*] It is the master builder himself?

MRS. SOLNESS.

[*Screams with terror.*] Yes, it is Halvard! Oh my great God——! Halvard! Halvard!

DR. HERDAL.

Hush! Don't shout to him!

MRS. SOLNESS.

[*Half beside herself.*] I must go to him! I must get him to come down again!

DR. HERDAL.

[*Holds her.*] Don't move, any of you! Not a sound!

HILDA.

[*Immovable, follows* SOLNESS *with her eyes.*] He climbs and climbs. Higher and higher! Higher and higher! Look! Just look!

RAGNAR.

[*Breathless.*] He must turn now. He can't possibly help it.

HILDA.

He climbs and climbs. He will soon be at the top now.

MRS. SOLNESS.

Oh, I shall die of terror. I cannot bear to see it.

DR. HERDAL.

Then don't look up at him.

HILDA.

There he is standing on the topmost planks Right at the top!

DR. HERDAL.

Nobody must move! Do you hear?

HILDA.

[*Exulting, with quiet intensity.*] At last! At last! Now I see him great and free again!

RAGNAR.

[*Almost voiceless.*] But this is im——

HILDA.

So I have seen him all through these ten years. How secure he stands! Frightfully thrilling all the same. Look at him! Now he is hanging the wreath round the vane!

RAGNAR.

I feel as if I were looking at something utterly impossible.

HILDA.

Yes, it is the impossible that he is doing now! [*With the indefinable expression in her eyes.*] Can you see any one else up there with him?

RAGNAR.

There is no one else.

HILDA.

Yes, there is one he is striving with.

RAGNAR.

You are mistaken.

HILDA.

Then do you hear no song in the air, either?

RAGNAR.

It must be the wind in the tree-tops.

HILDA.

I hear a song—a mighty song! [*Shouts in wild jubilation and glee.*] Look, look! Now he is waving his hat! He is waving it to us down here! Oh, wave, wave back to him! For now it is finished! [*Snatches the white shawl from the Doctor, waves it, and shouts up to* SOLNESS.] Hurrah for Master Builder Solness!

DR. HERDAL.

Stop! Stop For God's sake——!

[*The ladies on the verandah wave their pocket-handkerchiefs, and the shouts of "Hurrah" are taken up in the street below. Then they are suddenly silenced, and the crowd bursts out into a shriek of horror. A human body, with planks and fragments of wood, is vaguely perceived crashing down behind the trees.*

MRS. SOLNESS AND THE LADIES.

[*At the same time.*] He is falling! He is falling!

[MRS. SOLNESS *totters, falls backwards, swooning, and is caught, amid cries and confusion, by the ladies. The crowd in the street breaks down the fence and storms into the garden. At the same time* DR. HERDAL, *too, rushes down thither. A short pause.*

HILDA.

[*Stares fixedly upwards and says, as if petrified.*] My Master Builder.

RAGNAR.

[*Supports himself, trembling, against the railing.* He must be dashed to pieces—killed on the spot.

ONE OF THE LADIES.

[*Whilst* MRS. SOLNESS *is carried into the house.*] Run down for the doctor——

RAGNAR.

I can't stir a root——

ANOTHER LADY.

Then call to some one !

RAGNAR.

[*Tries to call out.*] How is it? Is he alive?

A VOICE.

[*Below, in the garden.*] Mr. Solness is dead!

OTHER VOICES.

[*Nearer.*] The head is all crushed.—He fell right into the quarry.

HILDA.

[*Turns to* RAGNAR, *and says quietly.*] I can't see him up there now.

RAGNAR.

This is terrible. So, after all, he could not do it.

HILDA.

[*As if in quiet spell-bound triumph.*] But he mounted right to the top And I heard harps in the air. [*Waves her shawl in the air, and shrieks with wild intensity.*] My—my Master Builder!